IF IN
DOUBT

WASH
YOUR
HAIR

ANYA HINDMARCH

BLOOMSBURY PUBLISHING

LONDON • OXFORD • NEW YORK • NEW DELHI • SYDNEY

BLOOMSBURY PUBLISHING
Bloomsbury Publishing Plc
50 Bedford Square, London, WC1B 3DP, UK
29 Earlsfort Terrace, Dublin 2, Ireland

BLOOMSBURY, BLOOMSBURY PUBLISHING and the Diana logo are trademarks
of Bloomsbury Publishing Plc

First published in Great Britain 2021

A catalogue record for this book is available from the British Library

ISBN: HB: 978-1-5266-2974-6; EBOOK: 978-1-5266-2972-2

2 4 6 8 10 9 7 5 3 1

Typeset by Newgen KnowledgeWorks Pvt. Ltd., Chennai, India
Printed and bound in Great Britain by CPI Group (UK) Ltd, Croydon CR0 4YY

To find out more about our authors and books visit www.bloomsbury.com
and sign up for our newsletters

IF IN DOUBT,
WASH YOUR HAIR

I dedicate this book to the women in my life:

To my family: my sister, my sisters-in-law, my mother-in-law (and hopefully one day my daughters-in-law), my god-daughters and my 'other daughters'.

To my girlfriends, the 'Women I Admire', the brilliant women I work with every day, the 'Walkie Talkies' and the 'Hormonal Voyagers' (don't ask).

Also, importantly, to the real mother of my oldest three children, her very supportive family, and to the incredible women who have helped me raise my children – especially the legend that is Mia.

But above all, I would like to dedicate this to my mother, Susan, and my daughter, Tia. If life is a relay race then my mother gave me a truly great handoff, and I am doing my very best to pass the baton as smoothly as I can to someone I know to be a very strong runner indeed. This is a bad analogy – running was never my strength – but I truly believe this baton pass to be the only really meaningful measure of my success.

CONTENTS

Introduction

I am often asked what my best piece of advice would be for a busy woman and I nearly always reply with: '*If in doubt*, wash your hair.' It's an answer that almost every woman seems to understand – at least, it usually elicits a lot of knowing smiles. On the one hand it is flippant, trivial. It literally sums up how much better I feel about myself – how much more confident, how much glintier-eyed, how much better able to cope and respond – if I have freshly washed hair. But on the other hand, I think my quip also speaks to the fact that we are all, and possibly women more than others, plagued by doubt. I suppose everyone who smiles knowingly at my silly piece of advice must also in some way relate to this doubt I'm referring to. I am fascinated by where it comes from, fascinated by how we can help ourselves to live our most doubt-free lives, and curious as to why it often takes until fifty to get there. If

I were to summarise what the rest of this book is about, it is quite simply that.

I never imagined that I would write a book. I am by nature an intensely private person and there were so many reasons not to put my head above the parapet and commit to paper for all eternity the jumble of thoughts that passes between my ears.

But, having hit fifty, I suddenly felt that I had a lot to say. Not because I have always got it right, but mostly, actually, because I haven't. And now I realise that that is OK too.

Turning fifty was a 'moment' for me: time to reflect and take stock. I had started a business aged eighteen, built it up until it had fifty-eight stores in ten countries, sold part of it, realised that that had been a mistake, and managed to buy it back again. I had come to a better-late-than-never understanding of the necessity (and surprisingly even pleasure?) of keeping my body and mind fit and healthy. I had, with lots of help, many missteps and much making it up as I went along, brought up five children in a modern blended family – not altogether unsuccessfully (I hope).

So I decided I was going to feel lucky, not resentful, to be getting older. And I realised how much I had learnt in my first half-century, and how much better it would have been if I had learnt it all earlier. I also realised that there are two issues on which the younger generation are shaming the rest of us right now. The first is the environment and sustainable living (more of that later) and the second is being honest about what goes on inside our heads.

It's funny, but when people first started speaking out about the importance of 'mental health', I remember wondering how it would ever be OK to talk about self-doubt, or to be openly vulnerable. And yet, quite quickly, the perception and understanding of the various voices washing around our heads has been transformed. From being something draining, misunderstood, unspoken of, it's now – for the majority of us – simply about remembering to look after our minds just as we do our bodies. Good days, bad days. A constant tension, some aches and pains, a continuing work in progress, a continuing inner dialogue.

But however good the younger generation are at talking honestly and sharing their feelings, they don't have the years of experience. And experience counts. I have noticed, when I give talks to groups of women, which I do from time to time, that the bits that resonate most strongly always seem to be the honest advice – when I share what I have worried about and how I have dealt with it, or not.

Covid-19 swept through our lives while I was writing this book. It changed so much, while at the same time reinforcing all the things I already knew. It emphasised the fragility of our planet. It made us stop and consider our core values and what was really important to us. It made horribly clear the overriding importance of looking after our physical and mental health and our families. It brought home to me how much good fortune I have had in my life so far.

Having reached this halfway mark, I thought I would put my fears to one side and share – as a mother to a daughter, as a friend to a friend – what I have learnt, what I worry about, what I think (rightly or wrongly) and the advice I have gathered, borrowed and stolen along the way. This advice covers thoughts on being a woman, a mother, a stepmother, a wife, a woman in business and an entrepreneur, and on dealing with the challenges that come with trying to keep them all going at the same time. I give it openly and, I hope, kindly.

At fifty I still feel the same as I did at eighteen. My father once said to me when he was about seventy, 'I don't feel any different apart from when I play squash or look in the mirror.' I think that is true. Except that also, I care less about the unimportant things. I have learnt to trust my judgement. And I have learnt to accept.

Someone said to me recently that until fifty you are learning, and from then on, it is your time to teach. It's almost laughable to see myself as any sort of teacher. But here goes.

Anya

I

'Anya, You Have to Take the Emotion Out of This'

Early in 2019, things at work were pretty tricky. I had sold part of my company several years earlier and stepped down as CEO, and the business had met a few bumps in the road. No blame and no finger-pointing, but it was a tough time.

It was during this time, however, that I had one of those wonderful 'watershed' moments for which I will be forever grateful. I was in a meeting and something was said by someone that was not fair, not right and went against what had been previously agreed. I called it out, in what I thought was a firm but measured way, and asked to discuss it privately after the meeting, which we did.

I will never forget the response. 'Anya,' he said, 'you have to take the emotion out of this.'

Woman are accused of being emotional all too often. Most of us immediately feel silly and girly and as though we have high squeaky voices. But I don't have a high squeaky voice, and I'm not silly or girly.

It is ironic that people will often fire that cheap shot precisely because of the emotions *they* are feeling, like embarrassment or guilt, when they have run out of any better ways to defend themselves.

This was a defining moment for me because what I have learnt and truly believe is that emotion is a female superpower and if women have an edge in business, it is in fact often because they *do* bring emotion to the workplace. A growing business is built on emotion. That moment made me vow never to take the emotion out of anything ever again.

Of course, I make an exception for anger – I always feel that showing anger is a sign of weakness. When I feel angry at work I try really hard not to react in the moment, and not to let aggression creep into the conversation. (People often overlook how aggressive it can sound just to use someone's name: 'The thing is, *Anya* . . .'). Better to leave it, sleep on it, and then to take the person aside when things have calmed down to explain my point of view in a more measured way: to 'use my words', as they say in the US. On the rare occasion – and I hope it is rare – that I've failed to disguise being angry or even made a slightly snide remark, I always feel I have let myself down afterwards, plus it sets off a pattern of behaviour that is contagious in the workplace. So I try to stop it in its tracks if I can.

Being kind and empathetic, being honest, even being vulnerable – keeping the emotion in – doesn't mean being weak. You can be kind but also be strong. Taking tough news, internalising it, dealing with tough thoughts are daily events as an entrepreneur. And being kind doesn't mean avoiding hard decisions. Of course, in a business – in any workplace – you sometimes have to make difficult decisions that are best for the organisation but not necessarily for the individual. As an entrepreneur, your first priority has to be the survival and success of the business, which of course is supporting the people you employ. This can be uncomfortable at times. But even with difficult decisions, you can make the right choice for the business but then find the kindest way to implement it and the kindest way to deliver the message.

Making someone redundant is probably the starkest example. It's a really horrible thing to do to someone, and also, by the way, a really horrid thing to have to do. Sometimes, though, there is no alternative. I have had to make people redundant over the years and I've found it to be the single worst part of leading a business – but it's possible to do even this very tough thing kindly and respectfully. You can take the trouble to explain why you are doing it and make it clear that you understand the implications for the person you are doing it to. You can commit to helping and supporting that person to find a new role as best you can and hopefully show them that it is not their fault. Sometimes you can even turn it into a positive moment of change for them: if it wasn't working, perhaps there's a reason that can be solved in a different way, in a different organisation. Above all, never forget to be kind, and never ever 'take the emotion out of it'.

There is a lot of talk in business about brand. In my opinion it's a really overused word. For me, the word 'brand' should be replaced with the word 'behaviour'. Your brand is simply how you behave, within the business and beyond it. You can define your brand all you like, but actually it means nothing if it is at odds with behaviour – with what is done and how it is done, repeatedly, day after day. I often think of a quote attributed to Ralph Waldo Emerson: 'What you are shouts so loudly in my ears I cannot hear what you say.' True, authentic behaviour – the patchwork of thousands of tiny experiences and moods and conversations and reactions – is much more important than clever taglines and catchy campaigns.

Today, having bought back my business, I think a lot about what matters to me and what attributes I want our company brand to be known for, both internally and as we face out to the world. And what matters to me most of all is kindness, treating people with respect and fairness, and being inclusive. Are they female qualities? Not necessarily. But let's celebrate them in any case.

I feel fortunate that I have never felt I had to 'behave like a man' – whatever that means – to progress. I have been lucky because founding my own business has meant the culture starts with me, and also because I have worked in the fashion industry, which is perhaps more positive about qualities that are traditionally seen as feminine than, say, the world of finance. I can see that it is not so straightforward for some people, but why would I want to try to be like a man? I love being a woman. I love being feminine. Do I want to be a powerful woman in a meeting? Absolutely. Do I want to be able to have a crack at everything a man would? Absolutely. Do I want to be treated the same as a man would be treated? Sure. But I don't want to have to be a man, or act in a way that someone says is like a man, to earn that. I don't want to wear power suits, or artificially lower my voice, or disguise my empathy, or pretend I don't worry like mad when my child is sick or sad. Let's all just be ourselves, not try to turn ourselves into parodies of something else.

I would also like to dispel the myth that women are particularly catty or competitive or territorial with each other at work. My experience is absolutely the opposite. I have always enjoyed working with women (and with men). I have a lot of women on my senior team. And I find women to be kind, intuitive, collaborative and resilient grafters who are right by your side when you need them. There are many men who have these qualities too: I for one would be lost without the men in my life. I'm not saying it's just women. I'm saying that women and men alike should harness and celebrate these qualities that are traditionally seen as – perhaps denigrated as – feminine.

I haven't found being a woman in business a problem. In fact, when I'm at work, I really don't think very much about being a woman – I think about being a person.

I understand that other women, in perhaps more chauvinistic workplaces, have struggled, and do struggle, but for me, in my business, there have only been one or two occasions – including the one I opened this chapter with – when I've really felt it has been a negative to be a woman. When I was in Florence, aged eighteen, looking for a manufacturer for my first handbag design, I ended up at a couple of very weird and inappropriate meetings in little piano bars. People in the finance world, perhaps, or in countries that still have particularly patriarchal cultures, will sometimes talk to my husband (and on one memorable occasion my son) more than me, but I just push on. After the first fifteen minutes, generally people realise I'm going to be making some of the decisions and start addressing themselves to both of us. And if they don't, then that's a flashing sign that the relationship is not going to work, so we move on.

What I *have* found to be challenging, though, is being a mother in the workplace. Balancing work and motherhood – or parenthood, I suppose, although it still does tend to be the mothers – is at times really tough, even if you are your own boss. There have definitely been moments when I've felt I am just not coping. There have been many testing weeks at work when I have had to say to the kids, 'You know, it's going to be a tough time, you're not going to see much of me, and even when I'm here I'm not going to be 100 per cent mentally here, but you just have to bear with me, we'll get through it, and we'll all have pizza on Saturday.' And there have been weeks when I've had to say to work, 'Look, it's the week of all the school plays, please cut me some slack and I'll make it up to you.' I remember getting an email from school once that nearly tipped me over the edge, along the lines of: 'Sorry, please ignore the request to drop your child at St Michael's at 7.50 with the lamb fancy-dress costume. Could you instead drop your child to the school boot room, but drop their fancy-dress tights at the church, but remember, drop the hat to Sophia's mum who lives at . . .' And that was one child, of five, all of whom had a Christmas show.

I have learnt that I have to over-communicate, be honest and make lots of lists – at home and at work. At home, we painted one wall in the kitchen with blackboard paint and we would put the schedule up on there so it was always clear who was doing what. Shared electronic diaries have made a huge difference: I heard recently of a (male) class rep who enters all the school dates into his diary and electronically invites all the class parents, so the dates automatically go into their diaries. What a star. Entering all those dates used to be a job in itself.

I try to include the children, sharing my work worries as openly as I can, as well as my work wins. I think they like to feel involved, and it helps if they understand why I'm distracted or stressed. I think it's important to explain what you're doing: that you're frightened, or struggling. It's tempting to try to hide it and not show that you are vulnerable, but I think it's better if children understand what you have on your plate. Whether it's 'I did it, I'm proud of myself', or 'Actually, I got that really wrong but I sorted it in the end', or 'It's nobody's fault, but it just didn't work out this time' – those are all useful life lessons for kids. It's when I forget to share what's going on, so I'm just feeling guilty and resentful and nothing has been articulated, and I'm communicating my stress only through mood and body language and how I react to things, that things go pear-shaped at home. It is hard for the children then, as they just see us looking at a screen, when in fact we're delving into hundreds of emails, each one making us feel a bit more anxious or overloaded.

I think it's important to accept that you cannot do everything, and to try to focus on the things you are good at. I've never really been a mother who's around for homework – and that's probably a good thing, as the truth is that the children are all more naturally academic than me. I have also had to accept that I am not a cook, which has been a struggle as my own mother is the most wonderful cook and homemaker. When I was a child, every bowl of Brussels sprouts came with sprinkle of toasted breadcrumbs and a chive tied in a bow. Yes, really. As an adult, I spent years feeling like a failure at the lack of chive bows in my children's lives. But I have come to realise that I show my creativity, and my love for my children, in different ways. And that is OK. I have to keep repeating that to myself, but mostly it is OK.

Finding the right childcare is paramount, of course – not just for the children, but for you. If you go to work feeling worried or guilty about how your child is being looked after, it is very hard to concentrate on your job. But even if, like me, you're lucky and can afford a nanny or an au pair, and even if you put the most amazing structures in place, and even if you're on a good run and find and hold on to the most loving, capable, committed people to take care of your children when you're not there, you will always live in dread of the five worst words a working mother can hear, usually communicated by email or text on a Sunday evening: 'Can I have a word?' These words mean someone I rely on – maybe my childminder, maybe my right-hand woman at work – is having a hard time of their own, and consequently something is about to fall apart. (I remember one nanny left me a 'Can I have a word?' note by my toothbrush, which didn't make for a great night's sleep.)

A short commute helps. Working with your husband helps. I know these tips are probably not all that useful or practical for everyone, but they were a big part of how I made things work so I'm sharing them nonetheless. They are, of course, a benefit of being your own boss: you can design your working life around your needs.

True one-on-one time, when you are 100 per cent given over to and tuned in to your child, is irreplaceable, but I don't think it's necessary as often as we sometimes think. It also doesn't need to be extraordinary or expensive. I listened to a podcast recently and the narrator talked about picking his child up from school: they played Batman together in the park, had a pizza, then he gave his child a bath and read him a story, and as he was turning out the light his child said it had been the best day of his life. Children know when you are 'for real' for them, and parents know when children need them. Parents and children are brilliantly programmed and attuned to each other. Trust the system. They will let you know when they need you (often through annoying and attention-seeking antics) and if they get you when they need you, they are pretty good at being self-sufficient in between times.

The toughest thing is how tiring it is. For years, as a working mother, you will just be so, so tired. For anyone like me who really needs their eight hours to function well, this is a big problem. Of course, it is almost impossible when they're babies. For those first few months, it's like going to an all-night party every night, with no weekends to recover; you get to Friday and it's no different. I am not sure there's an easy answer. My husband James and I called it the tunnel. You enter it, and it's tough, and wearing, but you somehow wade through it and are sort-of-happily spat out about two years later. I always wonder if working women like me are less good at this stage. I am so used to an organised, system-led existence that I find it hard to go with the flow and break out of a routine. I was often left in awe of my non-working friends who could balance a toddler over one shoulder while somehow also stirring a risotto.

This stage of motherhood was the single best and yet the hardest thing I have ever done.

The sleep deprivation starts up again when the children hit about sixteen. Suddenly they want to stay out until 'late' on a Monday night, just when you're prepping for an important meeting the next day, so you are not going to get any sleep.

For me, this was maybe the scariest stage of parenthood. Up until then I had always been able to find a way through. I had always been able to be there when they really needed me, and to make sure they were OK. But now I couldn't just wrap them in cotton wool and keep them safe at home with me, which is what I really wanted. Trying to find ways to navigate that territory together – to allow them their freedom and fun but in ways that didn't leave them in dangerous situations and me worried sick and up all night – was a huge challenge. We did a lot of talking. I tried to keep lines of communication open and to make sure they felt happy enough in their own skins that they wouldn't make bad, impulsive decisions to try to look cool. But I knew they were still vulnerable in so many ways: getting in the wrong car, trusting the wrong person. I still couldn't sleep.

My son Bert actually came up with his own solution for this. I put my dilemma to him: that I absolutely wanted him to have the best half-term, and that he deserved to go out and enjoy himself after his exams . . . but that this particular Monday was a problem as I had an important board meeting on Tuesday. I tried to explain that I was worried about him being a sixteen-year-old out in London until the early hours, and that there was no way I would sleep until he was home. I dearly wished I could (my husband can, and does) but I just couldn't.

It just goes to show, though, that you should try sharing the problem openly and honestly to find the answer, because Bert came up with a great idea that we and his friends' parents followed for years afterwards. He suggested that he could stay the night with a friend on

Monday, because his friend's mother didn't work so she could stay up to see them in on Monday night. Different parents could be responsible on different nights of the week, depending on their commitments, and I would be allocated Friday as I wasn't working at the weekend. Bingo.

When the kids were younger we did something similar in the long school holidays. I got together with some of the other school parents and said, 'Why don't we do a week each? I'll do the first week and look after the kids during the day and we'll have a fun time in London. I'll throw everything at it. They can stay with me the whole week if they want, and then the next week it's your week, and you've got them all.' It was a real solution for the working mothers and more fun for the kids too.

Another sleep solution that became a lifesaver was 'beat the clock'. The reason I am too scared to fall asleep when a child is out late is my terrible fear of waking up at 7 a.m. only to find that they are not in their bed and have been in A&E since two in the morning. With 'beat the clock', the late-night child and I agree a curfew (it can be late enough) and I set my alarm for that time and go to bed. The rule is that the child has to be back in time to turn off the alarm by my bedside *before it goes off*. If it goes off before they get home, it is well understood that they are toast, and it's back to a ten o'clock curfew. Of course, there is always a great deal of foot-stomping as the late-night child makes their way to the side of my bed, and the tell-tale boozy/smoky kiss is not exactly pleasant. But the reason it works for me is that I have a checkpoint. If the alarm goes off, there is a problem and I can do something about it immediately. I sleep much more soundly knowing I have this fail-safe checkpoint than if I were waking up a hundred times a night checking the time and listening for the door.

If babyhood is the toughest phase, this age, when they are experimenting, is the scariest. Technology is a help but also a hindrance. If you can persuade them just to text when they change locations, that can be reassuring. But the Find My Friends app (which a lot of people rely on, and which uses satellite location) can often be slow to re-locate. And then there is always human error. One night my son was, according to Find My Friends, 261 miles from where he'd said he would be. He was also refusing to answer my texts. This naturally led to complete panic and a sleepless night. Only the next morning did we discover that his phone had fallen out of his pocket and travelled to Cornwall in his friend's father's car. You also, of course, have to start to trust your children.

*

Whilst Christmas is my favourite family time, it is always one of the most demanding. Everyone dreams of making this day magical for kids and yet as they get older it is hard to get it right. There was one memorable evening many years ago when I was up way too late trying to finish my Christmas shopping online. I was struggling to work out what present I could buy for my nineteen-year-old that could possibly match the excitement of a £7 box of Lego that I had bought for the four-year-old. What is 'fair' as they get older? Setting the same budget or achieving the same sense of excitement? It wasn't possible to do both. I was exhausted and disgusted with the stupid waste of it all. In my panic I was buying things my son probably didn't need and using precious resource and time I didn't have. I felt there had to be a better way.

Which is when we came up with the idea of the 'Christmas Contract', something of which I am half-proud and half-ashamed. It started as a silly idea but it ended up solving a number of problems. The Christmas Contract was drafted by my husband in a sort-of-jokey formal legalese. (It was 'his thing', which made the kids love it even more.) For example, *'This document hereby sets out the Christmas Contract between the Parents (Anya and James Seymour) and the Child . . .'* It is now an annual contract between us and them (just the older ones at first but now all five) that states that each of our children will receive the same amount of money on 1 December, and that they are required to spend it in its entirety on Christmas presents of their choosing, for themselves, to be received on Christmas Day. (They are also required to buy presents for each other but that is not part of the Christmas Contract.) The purchases are to be sent home, unused and addressed to me. We provide some gentle present-buying guidance: '*As in previous years, you will be asked to think again if your presents appear ridiculous, pedestrian or just too dull . . . We will look favourably on new clothes, an alternative to that horrid red sweater, and, as last year, a high-quality electric toothbrush.*' I then wrap the presents, which are not to be seen until Christmas Day. The children are required to show '*complete surprise and joy*' in front of their younger siblings on opening each gift, and any unspent money is given to a charity of our choosing. My husband takes great care to choose the charity: last year it was the Fungus Conservation Trust, which looks after abandoned mushrooms (although I fear that the charity was untroubled by donations). The contract further stipulates that we would be thrilled to join them to choose the gifts (we have never been asked . . .) and that they are welcome to request permission ('*formally, in writing*') to save the money towards something that interests them ('*to be considered on a case-by-case basis*') – but not if it means they will then sulk on Christmas Day if they have nothing to open.

I know I will be judged for this, and I realise it is very much a privileged problem that isn't in the traditional Christmas spirit. But it was in the 'I am not coping and this will help me to get through' spirit and it has probably been more fun for everyone and less wasteful all round. The kids loved it and still love it. I don't stay up all night. They get what they want, we don't overspend our Christmas budget, it is always fair, and when I feel guilty I remember how much they enjoy looking out for the early-December sales to get the discount on the camera lens they want so that they can eke out every last bit of their Christmas Contract. It makes sense for our family, and has been a complete game changer. Sometimes it is necessary to make new traditions.

*

I think that is one of the big challenges of my generation of middle-class working women. For many of us, the models we absorbed through our childhoods – or that we were sold through the images we were constantly exposed to – were a father out at work and a mother staying at home, preparing delicious meals, organising beautiful birthdays and magical Christmases and generally running domestic life. At the same time we were encouraged to think we could have it all – the career, and the children, and the beautiful well-run home. But we weren't told how exhausting that would be and what a toll that would take on us. It's obvious, really. How can we do everything our fathers did *and* everything our mothers did?

If I am part of a 'transition generation' in which we women are trying to live up to our mothers' examples, despite now often working as hard as our fathers did; likewise men are often subconsciously following the patterns set by their fathers. Ultimately, things will get easier for working mothers as the home workload balances out. In my generation, women still tend to end up with the lion's share, not just of the childcare and the housework, but of all the endless admin that seems to magnetically attach to mothers: managing school dates, au pairs, uniforms, orthodontist appointments, picking up the sick child from school, and so on and so on. In my case this is (nearly) as much my fault as my husband's. I want to write that thank-you letter, as something deep down (from the example set by my mother) believes that 'that is what I am meant to do'. Meanwhile it doesn't naturally cross my husband's mind. We have discussed this a lot and we both realise we are stuck playing out old-fashioned roles. But, even knowing that, it is hard to break from them. There's a kind of behavioural muscle memory that is pretty powerful.

This has already changed in my children, from what I can see. My thirty-one-year-old son seems to split the chores fifty-fifty with his girlfriend. So I am very lucky with the men in my life – both my husband and my sons understand the need for change. Lady Brenda Hale, the former president of the Supreme Court, said it beautifully: 'Probably the most important thing when you are making your way as a woman in the law is to choose the right partner.' Sheryl Sandberg said something very similar in her book *Lean In*, advising young women to choose life partners who support their career aspirations. That includes by taking a fair share of the childcare, domestic and life admin workload.

I had a light-bulb moment a couple of years back when I received my first request for paternity leave. I have traditionally had a very female workforce and I always have two simultaneous reactions when a member of the team tells me they are going to have a baby. One is 'Oh, how wonderful, I am so absolutely thrilled for you', and the second is 'Help! How on earth will we cope while you're gone and how will we fill the gap?' I don't like to admit it, but I think if you ask any small-to-medium business owner they will say the same thing: maternity leave, and the kind of flexible working that women often want when they return from having a baby, is very hard to manage. Finding someone with sometimes very specific skills to fill a gap that might last three, six or nine months – because you don't know when they might return – is difficult. We always find a way and muddle through, by over-communicating and being honest and trying our best, but it's a challenge. When I was asked for this first paternity leave, I had the same two reactions. And then a third: 'Oh God, and now the men too.'

But then I had the wonderful realisation that THIS IS IT: checkmate! Paternity leave is actually the answer to equality at work and at home. When fathers have the same rights as mothers, and take similar amounts of leave, they are as 'inconvenient' to the workplace (I write this as a mother of five) as mothers are. Women have finally won this battle – and in fact everyone is a winner, including the child. Fathers get to connect in a different way with their children, children get to know their fathers better. And fathers get to do – or at least glimpse, and appreciate – the extent of that magnetic life admin too: the dentist appointments and the birthday party presents and the thank-you letters, not just the weekend trips to the swings. It becomes clearer to the men that it is not OK for women to work *and* shoulder all of that home workload alone.

The assumption that men can take Saturday morning to play sport with their friends, leaving the women to look after the children when we are working as hard as they are, is no longer fair. Every relationship is different and you work out the balance between you. But I still feel ashamed and lazy asking James to write a thank-you card for an event we have both been to. I'm definitely a work in progress.

2

If You Are Happy, Your Children Will Be Happy

A measure of the wonderfulness of my mother-in-law is that she only ever offered me one piece of advice. And it was a great one. She told me, 'If you are happy, your children will be happy.' She didn't mean me to take this literally: of course my children's happiness depends on many other things. But my mother-in-law's point was that making yourself unhappy by endlessly sacrificing your own happiness for the sake of your children is a mistake. It doesn't work. To be a good parent, you need to also pay attention to your own health, fulfilment and contentment.

A second invaluable piece of advice for family life actually came from someone with no conventional family of her own. From the age of eleven I was educated at a convent school run by nuns and I will never forget what tall, elegant, imposing Sister Angela said to us on our first day. She welcomed us all to the school and then said she was going to tell us something important. 'I am going to say one thing to you that I want you to really remember, girls. And it is this. *If you accept that you will never be fully satisfied, then you will be very happy indeed.*'

This struck me fully and deeply. It was like a balloon popped in my head: like I'd been inducted into something important about real life that my younger, primary-school self had been blind to. Don't expect everything to be perfect, Sister Angela was saying, and then you won't be disappointed when it isn't. It was a very generous life lesson to share with us and it has served me well.

These two pieces of wisdom have acted as beacons throughout my family life. They remind me to be realistic and not expect everything to be perfect, but also not to strive to make everything perfect. Getting everything 'just so' but driving everyone crazy in the process, and then seething with resentment and exhaustion about the effort, is not a great result for anyone. I try to remember that children – and adults, actually – remember the mood more than the detail.

It is a struggle, though, because it has meant that in countless ways I have had to make peace with not living up to my own mother's amazing example. I have realised that I can't and don't need to. I can quieten my mother's voice in my head. I don't need to make Instagram-worthy meals. Everything in my home doesn't need to be perfect.

This third piece of advice for family life is my own and it is the simplest. *Try to be kind.* Just that. But don't forget to be kind to yourself too.

*

I deeply believe in family: a strong family makes life so much easier. My own family is my tribe and my team and my foundation. A supportive family can act like a ready-made social services department, there for you when you're ill, if you're in financial difficulty, and in old age. The ideal is that you as a parent support the young and in turn they will support you when you are old. (And note that the way you treat your children as they grow up is probably how they will treat you as you age, which focuses the mind somewhat.) Not everyone is lucky with their family, though, and not everyone wants to stay with their tribe. Some people are forced to or need to move away from their actual family and create alternative families and support structures.

I know that I have been very fortunate. I am also very much aware that even with all of my good luck, making my family 'hum' has been a constant work in progress.

My first enormous stroke of luck was being born to two loving parents who were ambitious for me and supportive of me. They gave me the confidence to head out into the world, knowing there was always a warm welcome home to fall back on if needed. Parents, they say, are supposed to give their children roots and wings, and that is exactly what mine did. They also equipped me with helpful templates, when the time came, for marriage, parenting and being an entrepreneur. My father started his own business (in plastics, which is ironic as some of my biggest projects have been about reducing the use of plastics) when he was very young and my mother always says she was helping my father with an invoice when she went into labour with me. The family business was very much part of my young life.

Stroke of luck number two was meeting James, my husband, when I was twenty-five. However, this followed on from a devastating, life-changing tragedy for James: when I met him he had been widowed six months previously, aged just thirty-seven, with three children under the age of four. His wife, Felicity, or 'Flea', had tragically lost her life through complications from a routine operation. It was a heartbreaking scenario.

I am not sure how, but I knew the instant I met him that I was going to marry him. We had the same sense of humour, he didn't take me at all seriously, he was kind even though he tried not to show it, and I fell in love with his children.

James and I have managed (I hope) to create a loving family for my three inherited children, Hugo, Tia and Bert, and the two children we had together, Felix and Otto. Hugo, the oldest, is now thirty-one and Otto, the youngest, is seventeen and six foot four. I asked them recently how they thought people who knew us would describe our family, and between them they suggested loud, argumentative, boisterous, sarcastic, kind (most of the time), united (most of the time) and big.

*

I will never forget the first time I met my three oldest children. They were very little – one, three and four – and they were looking just adorable in their bubble bath. Three little soft heads. I said, 'Hi, I'm Anya', and after a bit James left the room and Tia said, 'Are you going to be our new mummy?' It was quite transactional for them. Children are straightforward like that, and pragmatic – they just want to be normal.

I'm not saying that their emotional scars from losing their mother weren't deep. They were: deep and lifelong. But they were keen for a new mummy because they were very very little and as far as they were concerned there was a vacancy to be filled.

Families have always come in many complex forms and these days it is easier to acknowledge that. When I married James in 1996, though, and suddenly became stepmother to three motherless children, blended families, as we now call them, were perhaps less common than they are today. It came absolutely naturally to me to love my three inherited children with all my heart. But I was completely unqualified. And when it came to the particular challenges of step-parenting, I was not aware of many models out there, nor advice about how to do it. Now I have lots of friends who, like me, are hugely proud of having made their blended 'modern families' work, and we talk a lot amongst ourselves about our stickiest moments and what we wish we had known when we set out.

James and I were extremely lucky to be very well supported by three sets of grandparents: his parents, Flea's parents, who were always fantastic to me, and my own parents. Plus James's sister Sarah, who stepped in when James was first widowed and was a complete rock. Looking back, I think all of us consciously decided – though no one actually said anything – that we were determined to make this work as best we could.

Certainly I was. It was a difficult enough situation and I didn't want to waste time on bad energy. I also didn't want to make the children have to choose between me and their mother's family. So we included all three sets of grandparents in everything.

The children, of course, were desperate to make it work too.

I remember one really touching moment when we were at a cousin's confirmation. Tia, who I guess was about seven at the time, was sitting between her grandmother Patricia (Flea's mother) and me. Tia took my hand and put it on her lap, which was nothing unusual. But then she put her hand on her granny's hand. And she gently brought Granny's hand onto her lap too, and put our hands together so that I was holding hands with Patricia. It was the most awkward and yet the most poignant moment: so natural to Tia and yet rather uncomfortable for Patricia and me. We both left our hands there for a bit and then after a while it felt natural to let go. But somehow it was rather significant.

Before James and I married, my own parents sat me down and said to me in a very kind way: 'This will be tough.' They said, 'Whatever is right for you is right for us, and we will support you and respect your decisions. But just think about this really carefully, because this is going to be difficult and you can't mess with children's lives. Once you have made this commitment, there is no going back. So this has to be really right. Parenting is difficult,' they told me, 'but step-parenting will be harder.'

Of course, they were completely right about this responsibility. And I was clearly working through the same issues myself because I had a particularly vivid and memorable dream in the run-up to the wedding where I was finding one of my inherited children really difficult and rude but I knew I had to just accept it because that was the choice I had made. When I went ahead and married James, that was a promise and a vow and a responsibility not just to him but to his children too. At that point they became mine. I was taking them on as my own, 100 per cent.

They were right too about it being tough. Parenting is hard, and I have no doubt that step-parenting adds another degree of difficulty. It's doable and hugely fulfilling. It's an honour and a privilege. Having created a happy family out of our difficult circumstances is the thing I am most proud of in my life, categorically. But do expect to have to work a bit harder. Despite the amazing support I had from three sets of grandparents, and despite having been given the best baton handoff you could ask for, it was often hard.

A lot of step-parenting is exactly the same as normal parenting: Look after yourself. Be united as a couple when you can. Row when you have to. Show your kids you can get through tricky patches and laugh about them afterwards. Have fun. Talk and listen. In its most basic form it's exactly the same: it's provision and it's love. But there are going to be additional complexities and challenges.

In my case the most significant additional challenge was that my three children had suffered a terrible bereavement. Our first priority was to make the children feel secure and loved and to dispel their fear that it was going to happen again, which was a risk that loomed large for them. We wanted to take away that worry as best we could.

Around the time we got married, Tia had a lot of nightmares, all different but always playing to the same fear. I was in the sea, and she was swimming too, and then a big whale came and ate me. Or she and I were in a zoo, and the lion bit my head off. It was always about her new mummy disappearing. We went to see the family doctor and asked whether we needed to go to bereavement counselling and she said, 'Actually, what this dream means is that Tia is starting to trust the world again. That's the time when all the worries come out. Until then, you are braced and shut down, but when you start to think things might be OK, that's when the brain allows you to start dealing with your fears.' She suggested that I explain this to Tia at the right moment.

A few days later, after another sequence of disturbed nights, Tia and I were in the car and I turned to Tia and said, 'Let's talk about this. You know, you're having the same nightmare every night, and while I can never say never, I think this is all going to be OK and you can relax. It is highly unlikely that you will lose a second mummy.' Amazingly, it was enough. She never had that nightmare again. Her little brain just needed to work it out. It was like a knot in her hair that needed combing through.

I wondered then whether we should comb through the other two children's knots, cutting them out if necessary, but the doctor said, 'No, it will come out for each child when he or she is ready. Don't force it. What they need now is to be normal. They want to get back on track, get back with their school friends, have a new family and for everything to be sorted.'

Children, she told me, are innately, brilliantly selfish. Childhood, when it's going right, should be a lovely, warm, fuggy tunnel that they slide down without really touching the sides, experiencing peaks and troughs and slight boredom. But my children had touched the sides and they were holding on tight. They needed to let go. They were desperate to just carry on with their lives. It seemed like good advice. We just carried on and muddled through and tried to make their lives as normal as possible.

My oldest, Hugo, didn't talk about it at all for a long time. Then one evening when he must have been about eight years old, he came down the stairs at ten o'clock at night when he should have been asleep, and told me, 'I've worked it out.'

'Worked what out?' I asked.

'I think the nurses must have killed her.'

Back we went to our amazing family doctor and she explained to us that when someone dies, their loved ones need to know exactly what happened, in minute detail, however good or bad that detail is. Then they can deal with it, grieve properly and move on. But with children, we protect them from that level of detail. It made me realise we needed to do much more talking, and we did, so they understood that everything possible had been done to try to save her. Later, when they were a bit older, we gave them access to everything, even the post-mortem report if they felt it would help. It was important for them to feel they had done their own inquiry, and that nothing was hidden or covered up, so they could achieve some peace with the situation.

In other blended families the children's biological parents are both still around and that generates its own very different challenges. Clearly it makes things easier for you and better for the children if you can say from day one that you are going to make the relationship with the other parent – and other grandparents – work. It is better if you can convince them that you're not a bad person and agree that you're all in this together for the sake of the children. Christmases and holidays get more complicated, but with plenty of self-discipline and generosity of soul they can be pulled off. From the children's point of view, that's just helpful. You have to remember that if you're saying something bad about one of their parents, you're saying something bad about half of the child. It is something that is so often overlooked.

There was another particular challenge when I had my birth children. James and I had deliberately waited a few years to let the older three settle into the new situation, but more children was something we'd both always wanted, especially as James is the oldest of five. The day I came home from hospital with Felix, my first birth child, James and I decided that he would take the three children out. Then I could settle myself at home, and settle the baby in, and when they got home I could give all my attention to the older children. We tried to be careful and thoughtful about the situation because we knew a new baby could make them feel threatened.

One thing that never worried me was the idea that I might love the new baby more than my existing children. I had chosen my three children, they were my first children and I adored them, and so I was not concerned about that at all. I knew it would be OK, and it was. So the added layer of complication, if there was one, wasn't from my side but rather from theirs. Each of them did a bit of testing at various times – *Have I got you? Are you going to let me down? Do I mean as much to you as this other child? Will you still love me even if I'm horrible to you?* – but I hope and believe I passed the test. I couldn't physically, biologically, be their mother. I couldn't pass them my DNA (nor would they want it, I suspect: their mother was a brilliantly bright and sporty woman with skinny legs!). But in every other way they are 100 per cent my children.

Relationships with grandparents can be complicated in blended families. Are grandparents – on both sides – going to naturally love their 'own' biological grandchildren more than their non-biological grandchildren? What is it reasonable to expect of them? These are very delicate issues. I always expected my parents to love all my children equally until I came to realise that I wasn't expecting that of Flea's parents. It seemed perfectly natural to me that they would love my older three a little bit more than my younger two. I think it's important to be realistic about the fact that grandparents and indeed parents are programmed to love their 'own' more. It's something I have chatted to my kids about. Having children and grandchildren is, in a way, the ultimate vanity project. It's about making another one of you. Hence all the 'He has your nose' or 'He has your big smile' or 'He takes after his grandfather.' This is nature's clever system, to make sure parents and grandparents don't abandon the child. Otherwise why would you take this tiny new stranger into your family and immediately put them at the top of your priority list, staying up for them all night and giving them all your worldly possessions? But with luck and commitment and honesty, you can achieve a very special and very happy non-genetic family. I think it's because you have *actively chosen* to adopt your children.

Sometimes, though, you imagine additional challenges when they are not actually there. Once, I was having a particularly difficult time with teenage Tia and I sat her down and said, 'Is this because I'm not your real mother?' And she just said, 'No. It's nothing to do with that. Of course NOT.' And I felt stupid and realised this wasn't about step-parenting, this was just parenting. She was just a perfectly normal teenage girl who was finding her mother unbearable in a perfectly normal way.

*

As a parent, you set the tone. You are the leader of your home team. You are the conductor of your little orchestra. When I'm grumpy or snide – and I do try not to be but sometimes I'm tired and resentful and cross and it's hard – everyone else picks up on that and gets grumpy and snide too. So you need to look after yourself. You need to keep yourself happy. You need to remember that it's not about creating a perfect table, or enforcing perfect table manners; it's the mood around that table that matters.

As mentioned previously, I am a truly terrible cook. In fact, while writing this book, I asked all my children what my worst parenting mistakes had been and the three older ones all immediately went to the time I tried to cook pasta for them and their friends. I was new to the family – James and I had just got engaged, maybe – and I was trying to be domestic and motherly. I had decided I was going to take Wednesday afternoons off work to be at home with the children. This was the first such afternoon and I had collected them from school and nursery, with a friend each, and successfully wrangled everyone home. Things with the pasta started out OK – just a simple tomato sauce, out of a jar. But it began to go wrong when I decided to freestyle (why?) and added various herbs and possibly also spices to the mixture. I also hugely overcooked the pasta, to the extent that it ended up a congealed mess that I had to kind of chip out of the pan. I knew it wasn't going well but I presented it to the children because I didn't know what else to do. They looked at it, and tasted it, and looked at each other. Then the assembled youth had a quick whispered conversation, after which Hugo, their spokesman, piped up and told me ever so sweetly and politely that their meal was not edible. 'We are very sorry but we can't eat this.'

'Sure, of course, we'll have toast instead,' I said. I do remember afterwards, quietly, privately, dissolving into tears. I was probably only twenty-six at the time and I remember thinking: *How am I going to become an instant mother to three children if I can't even cook them pasta?*

I did my best but it made me miserable trying to become the kind of kitchen creative that my mother had always appeared effortlessly to be. So I consciously reset my values and my expectations of myself. I was working full-time (the Wednesday-afternoon thing didn't go anywhere – I wasn't good at it and it messed up their routine), I had lots of children and something had to give. I decided that it was OK for cooking not to be 'my thing'. It is not my skill set and wasn't a win for anyone involved. Instead James – who absolutely loves cooking – cooked. Or our au pair cooked. Or I bought takeout rotisserie chicken from the place down the road. (To my shame/

pride, my children always refer to this as 'home cooking'.)
It was more important that we had fun around our table.
I did struggle with feelings of guilt and inadequacy but
eventually I convinced myself that it really didn't matter
whether I had cooked the food or not, and so I made my
peace with it.

Sports days have been a similar story. At the start,
when we had fewer children at school and fewer sports
days, James would prepare his signature onion tart and
grill sausages, and we would take gingham napkins and
make a picnic of it. A few years and a few small children
later, it became a packet of crisps, a box of sandwiches
and a bottle of wine that wasn't quite cold. We muddled
through, but we felt a bit guilty seeing the other parents'
marinated lamb on a portable barbecue. By the end I had
worked out that it was best to do one big, low-effort
thing well, ideally something funny or memorable. So
we would invest our budget into a big bottle of wine to
share amongst the parents, and nip to the cash and carry
to buy lots of tubs of Haribos and sherbet saucers, or a
huge box of Mini Cornettos. We would then set up an
after-lunch 'sweet shop' in the boot of our car, manned by
our children. No one missed the home-made onion tart
(my children never liked it anyway) or the napkins, and
the very simple sandwich lunch was forgotten. Instead
we remember the buzz of the queue for the sweet shop
and the fun of our kids doling out treats to their friends.

In general, we made a big effort to create memories of all of us together. Early on, we put a lot of emotional energy into throwing a big seventh birthday party for Tia (hosted by her brothers) and making it really special. It was nothing fancy but we called it the Spangly Party, and there was a lucky dip and a mixtape, and we went 'all in' in terms of energy. That still looms large in the collective family memory. These days it might be a family holiday or just getting everyone home and around the table for a big noisy supper. It doesn't need to be a big effort or expensive but it can raise the 'temperature' or mood of the family, and improve its cohesion, for months. The point is shared experiences, shared jokes, time together.

*

Childcare is a minefield. There are so many different approaches – and so much guilt, whichever approach people choose or rely on. Everyone seems to end up with their own personal mosaic involving grandparents, childminders, nannies, au pairs, nurseries, local teenagers, neighbours, friends.

I think parents need to look for an approach that works for them and then try to make their peace with it: try to zone out the endless newspaper articles or voices in their heads telling them they are doing it wrong and irredeemably damaging their children. And I think children will be fine if they have consistent, caring, enthusiastic care from people who are not (always) exhausted. If that's their parents, that's great; I might be shot for saying so, but children being looked after by their parents is probably the ideal as they have a personal interest in the outcome. But if that's not possible, that's fine too. Childcare is a really skilled and difficult job requiring a wide range of competencies: it's complex logistics, advanced diplomacy and tricky people management. Only, unlike in an office environment, no one tends to do what you suggest, and no one makes you a coffee, and a lot of your best work goes unremarked upon. Not everyone is cut out for it all of the time.

I love my children with all my heart. But I had other things I wanted to do as well and I would have been frustrated staying at home full-time. I needed another solution.

Maybe because I inherited three children all in one go, with no experience, I approached the problem like a project: *Right, this is actually impossible, I can't do it, how am I going to cope?* My approach was to imagine I was a British Airways pilot who sometimes simply wouldn't be able to get home, whatever the childcare emergency. I wanted arrangements with that level of robustness in place. That's not to say I really wouldn't rush home at any point if needed (and my office was only ten minutes away, which took a lot of pressure off): just that I needed arrangements that could cope when I was travelling or working late. And, ideally, I wanted arrangements that meant that when a child was ill they could still be looked after by someone they adored, someone who knew they would want the Mr Men plasters and knew which shelf they were on. I do feel defensive about it. Mostly because it cost a lot of what I was earning at the time, and a little bit because I worry that I missed out: they got fabulous consistent care from people who knew them inside out, but it wasn't me. I know I wouldn't have been as good at it as they were, and honestly the children now will say, 'Thank God you didn't stay at home, absolutely not' – but even so, I am their mother. I want to say I've made my peace with this but the truth is I haven't, quite.

If I wasn't the best at actually being at home with my children, I was at least very good at finding and hanging on to people who were. I put a lot into choosing our 'home team' and then doing whatever I could to make sure they stayed. We communicated hard, we supported each other, and we all became very close. I needed the people looking after my children to be people I loved, and I needed them to be fully invested in the family. Creating a lovely, stable childcare environment was a project in itself and the people who worked with us on that project remain close friends to this day.

*

Sometimes I think that every stage of parenting feels like the best stage when you are in it: when they are tiny babies who just need to be hugged and warm and fed, that feels like the best, and when they are three you realise toddlers are so absolutely sweet and much more interesting than babies, and when they are five and learn to read they are a revelation and a joy, and when they are nineteen you revel in your children having become such interesting adults, and when they are thirty you can go out for dinner and on holiday and they are more like friends. But at other times I think that every stage of parenting feels like the toughest stage when you are in it.

Certainly each stage of parenting has different levels of exhaustion, different levels of financial stress and worry, different levels of need.

When they are tiny babies, it's relentless, draining and crazy. I think people are more honest about that these days but even now people don't really like to admit that they didn't find it all wonderful. Then when children are toddlers they go to nursery or start to socialise, so just when they're starting to sleep through the night they get every flu and cold going. You go crazy trying to stop them tripping over and hurting themselves at every opportunity. You just have to grit your teeth and somehow get through it, and, once you are through it, be understanding with the other women still going through it. The only real comfort I have to offer is that I know it's hard but you do come out the other side (and of course you miss it as soon as it's over: I still crave having a baby falling asleep in my neck and a tiny hand holding mine when I cross the road). And the only bit of advice I really have to offer is to get help and protect your energy as best you can. Spend as much as you can afford on people to help you. If you have a mother or uncle or godmother or sister who can help, reach out to them. Get to know your neighbours and reach out to them too. Take a friend's child for a night, or for two hours on a Sunday, in return for them taking yours another time.

The other thought that helped me when the children were tiny was something my father said. Typical of my father, it's all in business terms, so it sounds rather matter-of-fact, but it is actually very wise. He said, 'Of course when you have a baby it's 150 per cent gain. There is nothing better. But, practically, you do also lose a lot when you have a baby: sleep, money, freedom to go out and do what you like. The adjustment you have to make to your life is significant. If, when you're pregnant, you anticipate only the gains that come with a baby, these losses are going to hit you over the head as a very nasty shock. It is the net gain that you need to focus on to have realistic expectations.'

As the children get older, the problems are different but in many ways just as testing. They need you less and less, but when they do need you the problems are more serious and harder to fix. At least when they're tiny they go to bed at seven o'clock and then you can sit down and eat dinner and have an evening. And at least if they fall down when they're three years old you can put a plaster on and make it better.

I found the teenage years difficult to navigate for other reasons: my lovely delicious babies started rolling their eyes and finding everything I did annoying and wrong. I started finding them annoying too: smelly and messy and ungrateful. One particular episode sums this stage up for me. I was with my daughter in Office, the shoe store, trying to buy her some trainers.

'Look, Tia,' I said. 'These are cool trainers. What do you think?'

And she flicked her eyes to them and just said: 'No.'

'Oh. Really?' I said. 'They're quite . . . I really think they're quite cool.'

'Mum.' Eye-roll. Eyes closed in exasperation. 'What do you know?'

And, slightly fed up with her typical teenage attitude, I'm ashamed to say that I said rather crossly: 'Um. Well. I work in fashion. In accessories. In fact I am Accessories Designer of the Year. So I really am qualified to tell you that these are cool trainers.'

Needless to say, Tia got the trainers she wanted.

A child psychiatrist friend really helped me through this while we were on an Easter holiday. I was explaining how hurt and rejected and even slightly bullied I was feeling (in general – it wasn't specifically about Tia or the trainers) and she was just so generous. She told me: 'Bingo, Anya, you've done it! You're being a proper mother to these children. What should happen is happening. Celebrate it.' She explained that children are meant to separate from their parents. It's a process that starts the moment they are born but it accelerates around the age of thirteen. Specifically in the case of Tia and the trainers, my Accessories Designer of the Year award was irrelevant because it was not about whether I was right or wrong. My daughter was just supposed to disagree with me, whatever my opinion. More generally, my friend said, you are supposed to become unbearably annoying to them, and they are supposed to become unbearably annoying to you. They are supposed not to give a damn about you. You are supposed to become good for nothing but cash and food and maybe a holiday. Otherwise, how could they ever bear to leave, and how could you ever bear to let them go? This has to happen to allow you to go from having a baby on your hip that you don't want to leave for an hour to saying, 'Woo-hoo! Bye! Off you go to university, see you in three months.' The children who don't want to leave – that's more of a problem.

Now that my oldest children are fully grown adults they find me much less annoying (I think!). But the parenting never stops. Their worries now are about jobs, or girlfriends: deep, important questions that sometimes have to be pulled out of them and which can't be resolved in the ten minutes between washing your hair and jumping in the car to get to work. These days James and I see ourselves as a kind of fancy garage for them. They arrive when there's a problem, download to us whatever is going on, fill up with food and sleep and family in-jokes, maybe get their washing done, and head off back into the world, all tuned up and refreshed and ready for another lap. It's what our parents kindly did for each of us and we are delighted to do it for them. It's lucky that we love them so much and need so little in return: as a commercial transaction, parenting would be untenable.

Whatever age your children are, talking, and listening, is key. That means telling them when you're stressed, and what's going on in your life – they love to be included, and they learn from it – and listening to them when they need you to. Honesty is also important: I think children really like it – and, again, learn from it – if you can own up to your parenting fails and say, 'This was tough for me and I felt I did it badly.' As in business, so in mothering. You go a bit too far one way, then you pull back, you apologise. You've got to be honest and tack your way through it.

Making children feel listened to, and that what they have to say matters, can be hard at the best of times; with five of them it sometimes seemed impossible. When the younger ones were struggling to make themselves heard above the eloquence of the older ones, and didn't quite have the words to fight back or keep up, we had to find a way to give everyone a chance to speak. We came up with a solution called 'the spoon', probably subconsciously inspired by *Lord of the Flies*. Even now, when things get out of hand and everyone wants to talk at once, we bring out 'the spoon'. Whoever is holding the spoon gets to talk, and to finish what they are saying without being interrupted, and everybody else has to listen. It worked really well to make sure the little ones were listened to and makes for quite funny mealtimes. Frankly, this would be quite useful in the office at times too.

When each child turned sixteen I tried to create some one-on-one time with them: a day or a short holiday. Those special experiences stay in the memory and can feed and sustain a relationship for a long time afterwards.

*

Of course, marriages need to be fed and sustained too. One night recently, James was helping me with a letter. I am very slightly dyslexic and he is a grammar bore so when I'm writing anything important, he will normally check it for me. No doubt he'll correct what I'm writing now. Or at least he'll opine on my grammar and drone on to me about my love for run-on sentences or some such. Anyway, James was correcting something that was probably fine and I joked that he was being 'my Denis'.

Meaning Denis Thatcher. Meaning my rock, the person on whom I can always rely. I then asked what I was to him and without hesitation he replied: 'You are my Margaret.' By which I know he meant a middle-aged battleaxe. How rude, I thought, but how typical. It's how we've rolled for twenty years. Affection from me and let's call it indifference from James in return. Endless sincere loving remarks from me, returned with a humorous jibe.

Luckily, I understand that humour is actually James's way of saying, 'Ange, I really love you.'

There is a weekly example of this, when, on a Saturday morning, I demand my marital rights in bed. By which I mean a cup of tea and the newspapers, obviously. And without fail, every Saturday, James brings me up a cup of tea along with the sports section of the *Guardian*. You might realise by this point in the book that I have zero interest in reading the sports section of the *Guardian*. But it makes me smile because, once again, I know that what James is really saying is: 'Ange, I really love you.'

James is humorous, light, happy in his skin and utterly unfussed about how he is perceived or what he wears. He lives in the moment and never ruins today worrying about tomorrow. As previously mentioned, he can talk to anyone about anything and he finds socialising nourishing and energising. These are all traits I am extremely envious of and they make him the opposite of me in many ways. We have very little in common in other ways too: we can't watch the same film, listen to the same music or read the same books. I can ruin pasta with tomato sauce while James loves to spend an afternoon planning and preparing an elaborate feast.

And yet we spend almost all our time together. We lie beside each other every night, drive to work together, and for the last twenty years of our working lives we've sat next to each other all day too. (James is a fellow director at Anya Hindmarch.) Together we have raised five children of whom we are desperately proud, and navigated some hectic moments and some tough ones.

I sometimes wonder how we did it.

We had good examples in our parents. And we both accepted Sister Angela's wisdom. Neither of us ever thought it would be perfect or easy. We were pretty realistic about it all.

I always say now to anyone getting engaged, first, that I'm thrilled for them, but second: 'Always remember this day. You have made a contract today.' If you were merging two companies, you would sit down with both sets of lawyers and do the due diligence and analyse the balance sheet and work out all the what-ifs and all the contingencies. For marriage you pretty much just smell each other (nature's way of checking your immune system compatibility, apparently), fall in love, and off you go. The smell of your immune system does the job of the lawyers and the contracts, to some extent. But you have to accept the balance sheet as it is today. If you find his mother annoying today, she's only going to get more annoying. Don't complain later. You know this today and it's part of the deal. If today he is handsome but has no money, that's part of the deal too. Likewise if he is rich but not handsome. That probably isn't going to change either – or at least if it doesn't, you can't complain. Be realistic. Note it today, accept it, realise it will probably get worse not better when the rose-tinted glasses come off, and don't moan about it once you're married.

If you don't go into marriage feeling pretty nervous and prepared for some hard yards then you aren't taking it seriously enough. Like everyone, there have been times when I've thought: *God, have I married the right person?* But then I thought: *Well, it doesn't matter. I made a decision. So now it's about making the best of it.* And naturally James has felt the same too. It is only human nature.

Of course, I do believe in divorce if a marriage is really wrong and things really can't be worked through. Because (as per my mother-in-law) I believe you have a responsibility to yourself and to your children to be happy. You are doing your children a disservice if they grow up thinking two unhappy people in a bad relationship is normal. But (as per Sister Angela) I also think you have to be realistic and reasonable about what happiness looks like. It is not endless bliss. And before you take the step of divorce, you have to be realistic about how much happier you will actually be afterwards. Not a week afterwards, but a year or two or three years afterwards. I have seen many examples, post-split, where the excitement of a new affair has quickly waned, and three years later the single parent is standing on the touchline with a third or fourth partner much inferior to the original. This plus the cost of dividing all the financial assets – and more importantly putting the kids through all the pain – means splitting up can net-net be worse than just doubling down and trying to work things out.

So I think your first responsibility is to work at it. You have to make the decision to make the best of it. When I'm getting irritated by all the things that were already in the debit column on our wedding day, I remind myself of everything in the credit column. And sometimes it is really nice to just sit down and watch our wedding video and be reminded of why I got married. Even writing this chapter makes me feel fond.

Part of working at it is actively deciding to spiral up, not down. It's the same energy either way, but spiralling down can make life seriously unfun. Once you start finding the negative ('I did the last nappy'), the negative gets thrown back at you ('Well, I've been up since five every day this week'). We all fall into the negative occasionally but I am working on trying to catch myself doing it. I remind myself that I have the ability to switch it the other way.

A lovely friend of mine taught me how to use micro-gifting to do this. (And, by the way, the positive spiral and micro-gifting techniques work for children, parents and work colleagues too.) It's not about buying your loved one a fancy new watch. It's more: 'I was walking past the butcher's and there were amazing-looking pork chops in the window. I know you love pork chops, so I bought you one.' Hopefully your loved one will pick up that energy and go with it: 'That's so nice. Thank you so much. You know what, you look tired – I'm going to run you a bath.'

Our marriage works through humour, through realistic expectations, through working at it and spiralling up, and – of course – through communication.

For example, James and I have had a lot of difficult conversations on the subject of forward-planning. James lives in the moment, which is one of the things that first attracted me to him. He finds it easy to relax and at the weekend he is very disciplined about switching off and not checking his phone, and he feels no guilt about it. But I am a planner and a forward-thinker. I find it difficult to live in the moment if the future isn't taken care of. So at the weekend I want to plan our family holiday and sort out projects to improve the house and spend time finding the perfect reclaimed taps. James doesn't want to engage in any of this. So we have had some tough discussions. I have tried to explain that the weekend is the only time I get to make things happen at home and that I would love us to do them together. He has explained that he doesn't want to do planning at the weekend; he wants to switch off. I occasionally manage to make him come with me to a car boot sale but it's usually more trouble than it's worth and I have finally come to accept that if I want to do this stuff, I am doing it on my own. By contrast, if I want a long and delicious lunch with hours of debate and quite a bit of ribbing, I am well served.

I also care about how things look: whether that's the number of candles on the table, or what the kids are wearing, or just not having piles of everyone's stuff all over the house. But James was just not prepared to budge. I don't blame him – in fact, I quite envy him, which makes it all the more annoying. So I have had to let some of that slide. But I can still flare irrationally when I come home to a house silted up with mess, or when a child arrives somewhere nice in one of those T-shirts that I had tried to sneak into the 'only to be worn as pyjamas' pile. These are silly examples but you get the gist.

Early on, we also had some difficult conversations about James's female friends. James has always had lots of really good girlfriends, and from the start that bothered me, absolutely unreasonably. It was an insecurity of mine and an irrational one. But I couldn't shake it. Finally, one morning over breakfast, I chose my words as carefully as I could and I said something like: 'If you go out for lunches with girlfriends without me, I'm not threatened, I don't think you're about to run off with them, it's just that I know that you will be your best self at lunch, and you will tell your best stories, and actually I'd like that time and that self and those stories. So I'm going to end up being jealous and, like water that can't be contained, it will leak out somewhere.' I said I knew I was behaving badly, but when he went out to lunch, had he noticed I was usually a bit of a cow in the evening? I said I would try to change, but that I wasn't sure I could. So could he change and carve out more time to spend with me, because I was worried it could end up being a problem? And to his credit, he did.

Every couple has its things, whatever they are. In a work situation, you'd be in with HR, drilling it out. In a relationship there's no contract but it's equally important to get it sorted, so that no one feels short-changed and resentment doesn't build up. I think that first period of dating and the early years of marriage are particularly important. That's when you pick your battles and discover your own red lines and your partner's immovable non-negotiables. It's about honesty, and talking, and listening. You have to see what you can give in on, and ideally find a sort of middle ground where you have both given a bit but have found a decent compromise.

For me, what helped to get through these times was to step back from my feelings and my knock-on bad behaviours and try to establish what was really causing them. I had to think, *I'm angry and jealous and grumpy and lashing out, but why?* and try to work out what the real problem was. And then find a calmer moment (three weeks later in the case of the breakfast chat about girlfriends) to lay it all out. 'I'm worried about this, I'm not coping, I'm bad at this, I don't think I can change this. Can you help me? Is there something you can give on?'

I'm a talker. I work out what I think by getting it all out, then picking through it. James would never voluntarily talk about emotions or feelings, but he is a kind, decent man. If I spell it out carefully in a considered, unemotional way, and present it as a shared problem that we need to solve, then he will engage. And maybe in the first engagement I won't even understand myself what's going on, and it will be more row than constructive problem-solving session, but then we will go at it again and eventually we'll get to where we understand each other and he can see my point and I can see his. It has become a natural way of proceeding for us and we have, so far, always found a way through. It's give and take. I gave on the car boot sales and he gave on the girlfriends. And so it goes on.

As parents, one of the most important things you can do for your children, I think, is to like each other. If they know you are basically getting on, that means they don't have to worry about you and they can go off into the world and focus on themselves. And it sets them an example that they can replicate.

Having said that, there are always going to be car boot sales and girlfriends – you are never going to agree with anyone about everything – so I also think that one of the most important things you as parents can teach your children is how to row. Forget a degree – this is what your children need in order to get on in the world. They need to see how you work things out when you disagree, how you express what you want and need, how you compromise, whether you blow big and then it's quickly forgotten (like James) or sulk (like me), and then they need to see that afterwards things are OK and most importantly you can get to the point of laughing about whatever it was. I was very generously handed that baton from my parents and I like to think that James and I have handed it on to our children too.

I see people daily who haven't been taught how to do this. There are proper grown-ups I see in a work context who have not been equipped to get beyond a disagreement. They don't know how to offer a critique without causing offence, or they don't know how to take feedback on board. They take offence, they become defensive, they dig in. And the issue becomes a scar. Either you have to cut it out if it's serious enough – by which I mean that person isn't likely to be a long-term colleague – or, more often, you have to find ways to bypass it. That inevitably means everyone tiptoeing around, aware that there are buttons that can't be pressed.

Five children later, and mostly getting it as wrong as I've got it right, there is one crucial role a parent has to play that I wish I had known about earlier. I was always ambitious for my children. I wanted them to work hard and do well and achieve, and so I thought my role was to push them and even maybe be tough on them occasionally. But something I believe now that I didn't appreciate when I started out is that, actually, if you just love your children to bits and make them feel incredible and confident then that is the greatest gift you can give them.

If you can smile at your children with your whole face, hang off their every word, find their (sometimes) terrible jokes funny, find them the handsomest, the prettiest, let them know you would step under a bus for them, and if they can go out into the world not cocky or smug but confident about who they are, happy in their own skins, liking themselves and knowing they are likeable, then that is an absolute win. That will help them to stay safer at parties. That will help them to drop all the defensive nonsense in an office context when someone disagrees with them. That will help them to express their needs and make good life choices.

It's not wrong to be besotted by our children. It's not wrong to make them feel like they're fabulous people. It's our duty, it's our job.

3

Put Your Own Oxygen Mask On First

I wouldn't consider myself a particularly nervous flier, but I drive my children mad by demanding that they text me whenever they are flying anywhere to tell me they have landed safely at their destination. The same drill when they come home. They moan and groan, but it is one of our family rules (one that I borrowed from my own parents) that has not changed even though the oldest two are in their thirties.

This ritual always reminds me of when I took them on their first flight and heard that classic line in the safety briefing which always takes me aback – 'Put your own oxygen mask on before helping others'. Every time I flew with them, I thought *Well, no, I'd never do that, I'd rescue my children first.* But many years later, I have come to appreciate that these instructions are right. It is not possible to rescue my children or indeed do anything very well if I do not look after myself first. I also now know, that the same is true in life. It may feel indulgent, wrong and often just not practical frankly to prioritise my own wellbeing when I have so many seemingly more urgent things to sort, but after years of experience I know it makes me a less resentful, more resilient, kinder, more useful human being.

In my life, stress has been the biggest threat to making this happen. It is the thing that if I am not vigilant can trip me up.

*

I went to see an acupuncturist once when I was at a low ebb. I had a mouth ulcer, I felt horrible in my body and exhausted in my mind. It was when the children were all small and I was just a bit wrung out. I had waited ages for the appointment, and the first thing he said to me was, 'Tell me about your life.' So I started telling him: I'm a mother, and a stepmother, and I run a business, and we have stores in this many countries so I travel a lot, and this, that and the other. Out it all came. And instead of sympathising, or being understanding, he said, 'Well, don't complain. Every single one of those things is something you chose.' I found this a bit hurtful, and then actually quite helpful (a bit like the acupuncture). A part of me felt annoyed but mostly I thought: *Actually, you're right, I did. And I did because I love them. I love my husband and my big family. I love my job. I love travelling and I love being busy.* I realised I actually even kind of liked being a bit overwrought. I like the building and the striving and the reaching, and the camaraderie that comes from it. Those hair-raising, nail-biting times are some of the best times, and some of the most fun and most successful moments of my life have coincided with the moments of peak exhaustion. There's something wonderful about pulling off a big new launch, then going home and tying 'I AM 4' birthday balloons onto the kitchen chairs in an exhausted blur at one in the morning. Keeping life full keeps it fun. The acupuncturist's insight allowed me to look at my life a little differently. I have chosen these things, or most of them. I have made conscious decisions to live my life the way I do. I could absolutely make different choices and have a different life but I don't choose to. So given these choices, it is then up to me to decide to be either the victor or the victim. All of this is something I am still working on, even now.

Like me, today's women are stretched. They are at home all day with tiny children or working long hours and travelling the world (Covid-19 depending) in demanding jobs. They are managing the home, organising childcare, supervising homework, taking care of ageing parents, writing the thank-you letters. Not everyone is doing all of it all of the time but most of us are putting in at least a couple of shifts as a matter of course. Often it's exhilarating. But sometimes it's exhausting and occasionally it's just unrealistic. Inevitably there have been times in my life when I've felt a bit overwrought, and I sometimes get to the stage where the weekend isn't enough time to bottom it all out.

Most people my age have worked out their own coping strategies for this by now, because for much of our lives these sorts of things haven't been openly discussed. For example, not so long ago, if you talked about your mental health, people looked at you very strangely and gave you a wide berth. Mental wellbeing sounded a bit indulgent, frankly, and we barely talked about mental illness at all: friends suffering with depression were 'a bit down'; schizophrenic uncles were 'a bit odd' or 'ill'. To the extent that we did talk about mental illness, we considered it to be something debilitating, permanent and shameful. There was little sense that mental health and physical health were two sides of the same coin. And little understanding that, just as we are all more or less physically healthy and can take various actions to look after our physical health, we are also more or less mentally healthy, and can, similarly, do a range of things to take care of our mental health. I have been very fortunate not to have suffered from mental illness. I do not have experience to share on that front. But like everyone else, my mental wellbeing is a work-in-progress and there have been better times and worse times. For me, this has mainly been about stress and exhaustion. I have had to learn to prioritise my mental health as well as my physical health: how to deal with exhaustion and stress when I'm right there in it, and how to try to stop myself from getting there in the first place.

I have found that stress is so often a question of perspective. Many years ago, for one of our Fashion Week presentations, we created an Ames room: an optical illusion where people appear very large or very small depending on where they stand in the room. I often think of this room when I think about how stress works. I see each person's level of stress as a zero to ten on a scale running up the wall of a room. The zero mark is at floor level and ten is on the ceiling. Each person is functioning inside their own stress-room and they grow and shrink according to how stressed they are. If I am at a level five of stress, I will be at a normal kind of size within my stress-room, going about my life and functioning perfectly well. A moderate level of stress suits me just fine: I would be bored without it. I like being busy and I like trying to do challenging things. But if something pushes me up to a nine, things start feeling quite claustrophobic, and at ten my head is bumping up against the ceiling and it's hard to cope.

I also think, though, that even if on some kind of objective measure people are subject to radically different levels of stress, each person can feel they are operating across the full range of their own scale. I realise that my life at its most stressful and exhausting is a walk in the park compared to the life of a junior surgeon performing life-saving operations on not enough experience or sleep, or a refugee trying to keep their family fed and clothed and safe. I also know that there are lots of people out there feeling very anxious about situations that would barely register on my stress-o-meter. My grandmother used to call me to say she was very worried because the electrician hadn't turned up and also she had to bake three cakes for the church fundraiser. She would genuinely be feeling very stressed about it – she would be feeling like she was at an eight. And I would be thinking: *Bless, poor thing!* But also: *Really? I've got Fashion Week and a major board meeting coming up and three children on half-term.* And perhaps you are reading this thinking: *Fashion Week and a board meeting and half-term? Bless, poor thing!* But also: *Really? Try being me.* It actually doesn't help me very much to know there are other people who have more of a right to be stressed than I do; or even that I have lived through much more stressful situations than whatever feels stressful to me today. And I don't think it would have helped my grandmother if I had told her to stop worrying about the cakes because I had Fashion Week. I respect that she was at her eight and it felt as bad to her as being at my eight feels to me. All I could do was recognise that she was telling me how she was feeling and was asking for support. Stress is not something else that we need to compete over. That said, do remember to ask for help and tell people how you're feeling. The people who love you will want to help you if they know you are struggling. Sometimes it takes just one night off from young children, just one evening laughing and letting off steam with friends, or just one big download with a close friend who will listen, to protect your energy and give you the break you need to keep going.

Fashion Weeks and board meetings can be stressful but they actually do not feature in my list of most difficult times. The first of these would have to be just that magical but depleting period of having little children. For so many people this is a time of relentless exhaustion. The days are long and demanding, and there is a blurriness to the broken nights. We're forging our careers, maybe we've taken on a mortgage to house our growing families, we have heavy outgoings, we don't have the time to keep ourselves physically strong. Whether we're doing all the childcare ourselves or managing other people to do some of it, the child-related logistics often fall to women – or at least they did when I was at this stage – and they can be brain-frying. We are just getting through and it doesn't take much for things to suddenly spiral out of control and for life to feel completely unmanageable. Second: a really tough and scary time at work. I was consumed by it during the day and waking up with it at night. I forgot how to switch off and for months and months I was awake at four o'clock every morning. Third and worst: when my eldest son became seriously ill ten years ago. The stress was almost unbearable. That was on a different scale to anything else before or since.

For all those challenging moments, and whenever anything stressful comes up now, I rely on the same strategies to get through. The first is to deal with the physical and for me that means addressing the basics: breathing, exercise, food and sleep. When I get stressed and overtired, I stop functioning as I would want to. There's an immediate physical reaction – sometimes perhaps a mouth ulcer or swollen glands and the letting go of good intentions around exercise and healthy eating. Also, if my stress level is raised, I notice that my breathing can become shallow in a form of hyperventilation. I become overly aware of this function that I normally automatically manage every moment of every day. I find it hard get to the top of my breath. It really helped when someone taught me how to properly exhale. This helps in any anxiety-inducing situation: a job interview, a scary meeting, a daunting presentation: any time your heart starts thumping and you become uncomfortably aware of your own shortness of breath. It's also effective for dealing with other emotions like anger or frustration. The key, of course, is to take deep, slow breaths. But the trick I learnt is to focus on the out breath, not the in breath. It feels, when your breath gets short, as though the issue is getting the air in, but actually it's about getting it out. If you really focus on emptying your lungs with every out breath then the in breaths will start taking care of themselves. It's interesting that when you go to bed and settle down to sleep, often the first thing you do is a big exhale. It's the first thing you need to do to relax.

I was taught that this kind of breathing is a very basic form of autogenic training – a technique developed by the German psychiatrist Johannes Heinrich Schultz, by which we access our body's physical relaxation processes and use them to relieve stress. When I was a child and couldn't sleep, my mother taught me another version. She would sit by my bed and tell me to feel the weight of my head sinking into my pillow; to clench my jaw as hard as I could, then relax it; then to clench my fists and let them go. We would work through my whole body, clenching and relaxing, but usually I was asleep before we got beyond my shoulders. I used to do the same thing with my children when they couldn't sleep and within about half a minute, I would hear their breathing slowing. It's a powerful thing. I have sometimes used this technique in the middle of a working day if I'm back-to-back and feeling the pressure, just to take a moment to reset myself. I mentally scan my body. *How are my shoulders feeling? My neck? My forehead? I can relax my jaw. I can drop my shoulders. I can feel how heavy my hands are. I can feel how heavy my hips are. My knees, my ankles.* I scan my body twice. I feel a bit of an idiot doing it, but in five minutes it can take my stress levels right down. You can even do it in a meeting while everyone else is talking. Other people meditate and achieve a similar effect. I'd love to be able to do that, and I know relaxing your brain is important, but I find it very difficult; I think it's because at some level I love the stuff that's going through my head and I don't want to let it go. But focusing on my breathing, and on how my body is feeling, is another way of making myself pause, stilling my internal chatter, gaining some perspective and – at its best – taking a moment to just stop and be.

*

It has, though, taken me until now, aged fifty-two, to understand the concept of getting a buzz from exercise. I wish I had grasped it earlier, because I've missed out on decades when I could have been buzzing and wasn't. I was unsporty and uninterested in sports at school. My parents tried hard to encourage me but I was impressively resistant. (I was, however, an accomplished smoker, which was the alternative sport at my school. The nuns who were in charge decided, since they couldn't stop us, that at sixteen we were permitted to smoke on 'the smokers' bench'. I certainly put my back into that particular sport.) And in those days, if you didn't do actual sport, you tended not to exercise at all. There was less understanding of how important it was. When I hit my late teens and early twenties it was the mid-1980s. Aerobics was a thing, and I did a lot of that. I liked that it wasn't a sport and I liked the social aspect of it. I did build a bit of fitness then – I put some credit in the bank. But I was also crazy-busy starting my business, and I was probably going out most evenings and not eating very healthily. Not in an out-of-control way but just in a sloppy, this-is-what-we-do-in-the-evening-when-we-are-young way.

Pretty soon afterwards, I hit the insanity of having lots of small children. This was a source of enormous fulfilment and joy. But it became very difficult to find the time or the bandwidth to exercise. It was all I could do to get everyone out of bed and out of the house, into the right place at the right time with the right stuff. It was, in the nicest, most love-filled kind of way, relentless. Getting to the gym before work was completely out of the question. I would have felt better and more energised if I'd carved out the time to walk, or get to an exercise class.

But it felt impossible. It's hard to find the answer for those who are still in that bubble. The dream, I suppose, is to find ways of exercising with your children. Walk or jog while pushing the buggy at the weekend. Quick-march them to school instead of driving. I rarely managed it and I don't think many people do. So the more realistic solution is to have paid some strength and fitness into your personal body bank before the children arrive. These days, things are different for me. My oldest children are adults and even my youngest is a teenager who can get himself dressed and out of the house without assistance (most of the time!). I have time to do more things for myself.

The thing that really changed exercise for me was very simply starting walking. First of all, it's free. And I do it with a girlfriend, which is a game changer because it means even if it's raining, it's in the diary, I've made a commitment to my friend, I can't let her down. I also love that it's multitasking because of course we talk as we walk, so it's a wonderful opportunity to offload and discuss anything on our minds. My son is always teasing me: 'Have you beaten your time? Did you introduce any running?' But although we do occasionally break into a run, it's not like that. That would work for him but not for me. What I've found is a form of exercise that I enjoy and I don't give up. So for the last eight or nine years I've been walking with my friend, early in the morning, for one hour, three times a week. There is lots of good evidence that even a short walk near some trees in the morning sun can improve your day, and it certainly works for me. By 8.30 in the morning I've done my 10,000 steps, I've been outside, I've cleared my head, I've had this precious time with my friend, we've talked through whatever is on our minds that day – not business, but husbands, kids, worries, all of that stuff – I've got my blood pumping and I have that incredible buzz of well-being that is part feeling virtuous and part circulation. My mood is massively altered for the rest of the day.

The walking was the way into everything else. It made me feel fantastic, and the more I did, the more I wanted to do. I started going on afternoon hikes when I was on holiday with friends, up and down hills: bright pink in the face and huffing and puffing and taking lots of breaks on the first day, striding and pushing and euphoric by the end of the week. I never believed in exercise euphoria – I thought it was a myth – until I experienced it. It's quite a subtle high, but it lasts a long time and once you start to experience it you don't want to give it up.

More recently, I've been trying to get to the gym twice a week, to do the strengthening exercises that have completely transformed my back, which was damaged from lifting something heavy when I was pregnant. (A can of paint, when I was in that frantic nesting phase and decided I absolutely must sort the attic today.) Back pain is a source of amusement to everyone who has never had it. But anyone who has ever had chronic back pain knows that it is boring, and draining, and changes all sorts of decisions you make about how to live your life. It used to be the case that if I went on a long flight, it took me two days to recover. And now, after less than a year of the gym, I would say I am cured. I still wouldn't say I love the gym but I do love its effects. For me it's like the Nike slogan: *Just Do It* . I just have to put my trainers on and get out of the door. And once I do, I feel dramatically better. We all know this but it's so hard all the same.

It always makes me laugh that when I'm doing regular exercise, I can't imagine ever not doing it because it makes me feel so good. And yet when I'm not doing it, I can't imagine ever doing it because I forget how it makes me feel and just remember the time and effort it takes. (I sometimes take a selfie of myself and my friend after we exercise so I can remind my future-self-who-has-spiralled-down-and-given-up-exercise how good it makes me feel, and I always look really happy in those pictures.) But now I hope I've got myself to a point where exercise is so much a part of my routine that I won't ever stop. I've found my forever thing.

*

Food is more complicated. It is, in my experience, rare to find a woman with absolutely no issues around food. And that's because our issues with food aren't really issues with food: they are issues with feelings and emotions, and what food has come to mean to us, whether that's comfort or love or guilt or reward or control or lack of it. We use food to celebrate, to punish, to motivate. I know that for me, food – or more specifically sugar, or even more specifically Maynards Wine Gums – is about stress. It's what I go to when I'm under pressure, when

I hit that dip. The whole studio does, actually: when we're on a deadline, the whole office switches to living on strawberry laces from the newsagent next door that are filled with white sugar and come with a health warning saying they alter children's behaviour. I once, in an idle moment on a plane, plotted my weight against the times in my life when I've been most stressed (I had bought myself electronic scales that sent my stats to my phone) and the two metrics were perfectly in sync. Incidentally, my husband said that he knew this to be the case. When I asked him how, he revealed that the bathroom scales were sending my weight and stats to his phone too. Oops.

I've done a lot of thinking and reading about it because it puzzles me. I'm a pretty disciplined person. I work hard, I'm committed, I stick to what I say, I'm reliable, I deliver. And yet when it comes to food, it's different. If I'm on a deadline, or travelling endlessly, or flat out at work when it's particularly busy at home too because it's half-term or Christmas, I lose that self-control. Sugar actually calls to me. It's really noisy. I can hear it from another room. I remember one defining moment for me was when I had been to a meeting that had overrun and by the time I got back to the office it was 3.30 p.m. I hadn't had breakfast, and I hadn't had lunch, and I found myself frantically rifling through everyone's desk drawers looking for something sweet. You could have cut my arms off and you wouldn't have stopped me. I had to have sugar.

I've come to understand that the problem is that sugar is actually a pretty effective coping mechanism in stressful situations. It's instant dopamine. It's a quick hit of security and comfort as well as energy. Plus, on top of being instantaneous, it takes almost zero time or effort out of my busy day, it's cheap, it's legal, it's readily available and it doesn't hurt anyone else. I can still drive, I can still do my job, I'm not going to start behaving oddly. However, I also know that after the quick sugar hit will come the crash and the cravings for more: up, down, up, down. I know the insulin spikes are bad for me. I suspect everything about refined sugar is bad for me. But it is incredibly addictive – as addictive as cocaine, they say. It's upsetting to me that sugar is my Achilles heel, but I find it very helpful to understand why it calls to me so loudly. That understanding allows me to be a little kinder to myself, to cut myself some slack. Rather than feeling completely shamed by my sugar lapses – shame is never particularly good motivation – I can remind myself that I've found an easy way to get myself through sticky patches. Not a consequence-free way, and not something I'm proud of, but it's my crutch when I need it. It's pretty effective and it's better, perhaps, than some of the scarier alternatives. But, of course, there are alternatives that are so much better than sugar: going for a walk, getting more sleep, a strong coffee. Caffeine doesn't actually give me that same boost, though. (I wish it did.) A walk takes an hour I don't have when I'm on a deadline. Ditto more sleep or talking things through or playing the piano or reading a book. A massage costs time *and* money. My husband turns on the TV when he wants to relax or get that feeling of comfort that I get from sugar. Crappy TV numbs him and relaxes him. My brother, meanwhile, goes for a run.

I doubt that I am ever going to find comfort in going for a run. But I am, gradually, with lots of slips because it is really hard, reprogramming myself to get my lift in mood and energy from alternatives to sugar. It's not so instant. It does take time and effort. The buzz is not quite as immediate. But there's no crash, so net-net it's better. So, if you are, for whatever reason, perhaps to do with your childhood, programmed to turn to sugar when you're stressed (or tired or sad or happy), cut yourself some slack. There are good reasons why sugar is such an attractive option. You've found an instant way of soothing and comforting yourself and getting through. If you need strawberry laces to get the kids organised and the job done, that's OK. But also, would it not be great to reprogramme yourself, to find other sources of comfort, and also to programme your children to have other comfort blankets? To separate nutrition and emotion for the next generation? Of course, yes. And I find it helps to remind myself to make sure I'm looking after myself as well as I would look after my children. Would I feed them sweets that come with a health warning? No, I would not.

*

Someone once asked me what I was most scared of and I only half-jokingly answered, 'Not getting enough sleep.' The reality is that a tired me is about 10 per cent of what a not-tired me can be. If I don't get enough sleep it affects my mood, my resilience, my self-discipline and my immune system.

When I'm tired, I can no longer prioritise, and I lose both my sense of perspective and my sense of humour. At my most strung-out and sleep-deprived I have been known to start writing to-do lists that say things like: 'Get up. Have shower. Eat breakfast.' Even I know this is not a strong to-do list system. I just get to the point where I'm so exhausted I can't even fathom what is automatic and what needs conscious thought. A list that tells me 'Get up' is a flashing red light that I should go to sleep and start again in the morning, but by that point I may have lost the ability to read the signs.

There is still a lot to discover about sleep and how it functions. I recently attended a fascinating lecture on sleep by Russell Foster, Professor of Circadian Neuroscience at Oxford University, and I learnt that when people are very sleep-deprived they can only lay down negative memories into their long-term memory. Knowing how low and negative my mood gets when I'm tired, that rings very true to me. A big late night out basically costs me my next day. It is often worth it, but I have to accept the trade-off. It's so tempting to cram the diary full of school events and exhibitions and dinners along with the work events and trips, all of which I find exciting and inspiring. But I know that if I have lots of late nights I will 100 per cent pay the price (as will the family). Someone once gave me some wise advice: 'Don't accept anything that you wouldn't want to do tonight.' It was a bit sobering but in many ways quite sensible, especially as I hate to be that person who cancels at the last minute. That said, I have a very dear and brilliantly ruthless friend called Kate who often tells me, in the kindest possible way, 'No one cares. Get over yourself. You're not so important that your absence is going to ruin everyone's night. And there's always next time.' She is probably right, but I still don't like to cancel.

My choice of career hasn't helped with my sometimes erratic sleeping habits. I travel a lot for work (or did pre-Covid), often quick and busy three- or four-day trips without much of a chance to acclimatise. Jetlag for me feels a bit like a low-grade flu, but at a dinner many years ago in Korea I sat next to the publisher of the *International Herald Tribune*, who gave me some amazing advice. He told me that to get through that 4 a.m. itch where you wake up raring to go and curious to check your emails, only to suffer a complete collapse a few hours later, you should go to bed at the normal local time but set your

79

alarm to take half a sleeping pill at two in the morning. Instead of taking a full dose at eleven in the hope that it'll get you through the night, you take half a dose at two, which is better for you but also keeps you asleep through the 4 a.m. danger zone. I hate taking sleeping pills (and only do so for a maximum of three nights at a time) but I follow his advice religiously now and it works. It is a big improvement on the time when I was in Asia and was asked to make a speech at the Condé Nast Luxury Conference. I had such bad jetlag the night before that in desperation I took a sleeping pill in the 4 a.m. danger zone. I made the speech but have no memory of it *at all*, nor any memory of Kate, my brand director (a different Kate, though similarly dear and brilliant), taking me to an anteroom beforehand and making me drink three espressos and a Diet Coke to try to wake me up. I am not sure it was my best speech but I look very happy in the official photos taken in the green room afterwards, albeit a little cross-eyed if you zoom in closely.

*

As well as getting enough sleep, I have found that I have to treat myself as I would treat my phone and make sure I manage my batteries. I have had to learn to identify the things that I feel I ought to enjoy but which actually just drain me; and to distinguish these from the things that actually give me pleasure and recharge me. It is important to be honest with yourself about what makes you happy. An evening at a fancy party can sometimes leave me tired and depleted. A cup of coffee and a walk with a girlfriend often brings me deep, real happiness. It has taken me years to understand, for example, that I find small talk utterly draining (and I'm not very good at it). I would rather negotiate a contract, frankly. A good example of this for me is a drinks party – the kind where you stand around in little groups, mostly having unmeaningful conversations. My friend calls it 'tiny talk'. I always feel a bit trapped. I feel the person I'm talking to is dying to get away and talk to someone else, but I don't want to move away or do anything to imply that they should move away, because I don't want them to be left on their own, or to think I'm bored with them. So I end up stuck, and not knowing how to leave, and boring even myself. It drains my batteries completely. If I do it for an hour I feel like I've given blood. Whereas a good sit-down dinner and a meaty conversation I find totally nourishing. Thankfully my husband is brilliant at tiny talk. He can talk to anybody for hours about anything: at a drinks party, at the barber, at a work event. I'm very envious: it's an incredible social skill that I wish they taught at school. Perhaps this is why we're a good match.

*

The next most important consequence of stress is dealing with the mental reaction. In challenging times I keep going, but I become a bit intolerant, a bit irrational. I am less able to handle the little things that wouldn't normally trouble me. I call it 'doing dominoes', because it reminds me of our 2013 London Fashion Week Show 'Cascade'. The show involved 50,000 dominoes set up in an ambitious, Willy Wonka-esque creation where each domino would fall and trigger the next one. It was torturous to build, as knocking over just one tile at the wrong time would ruin the whole show, but it was magical on the day. For me this show is a visual representation of how if I am not careful, I can let one thing affect something else that's completely unrelated: a problem at work affects how I behave at home, or vice versa. I know that, as a good, respectful adult, being snappy with the children because a delivery deadline has been missed at work is not a productive way to operate. I should not allow myself to do dominoes. But I am prone to it under these circumstances. If I'm upset it is easy to become immersed in whatever it is that's bothering me. It is less easy for me to just switch off or put it in a box. Some people are really disciplined when it comes to dominoes and compartmentalising their lives. I know people with highly stressful, properly important jobs who are able to say: *You know what, it's Friday night, let's forget about work, open a bottle of wine and cook a delicious dinner.* My late and beloved aunt Elizabeth managed her cancer treatment that way. She told me, 'I put it in a box and I tie it up with ribbon and put it on the top shelf, and I don't bring it down until I need to. I carry on. When it's the next medical appointment I take the box down and deal with it, then I put it away again.' How I envy that ability.

I could be better at compartmentalising, but something that helps me is to just simply write down all the things that I'm worried about so that they're out of my head and onto a list. I do it on my phone, which means that as I do it I can see my previous versions. That in itself sometimes helps, because I look at the old lists and think: *Well, that was a ridiculous thing to worry about.* Or: *That was pretty easy to sort.* Or sometimes: *What does that even mean?* Often I just can't remember the thing that was eating me up eighteen months ago. But even if looking at the old lists doesn't help – sometimes I genuinely believe nothing has ever been as stressful as this is right now – the very act of writing it all out helps. It is not putting it in a box in a cupboard but it does feel like everything is set out neatly on open shelves. I can survey it and get its measure. And I have at least put it down.

I have also started to actively look for things that will take my face out of my phone. The other day I found myself booking to go on a bread-making course, which is a curious idea because I hate cooking and I'm trying to cut down on carbs. But it speaks to a yearning I think a lot of people have, to put down our screens and do something that feels more real, more earthy: to do something with our hands, learn about craft, understand how things are made and be more mindful of how we use resources. Apparently you cannot get a place on a pottery course in London for love nor money. It was the same thing when we did an art installation for London Fashion Week to promote a woven leather bag. The installation was about weaving, and people who visited it could clamber through a huge woven structure we had built. But we also had lots of information about the subject of weave, and we had the product there, and we showed people how we did it. And then we started showing people how to do it themselves. At one point we had eighty or ninety people sitting on the floor weaving. We hadn't planned that. We would have had chairs there if that had been the plan. But there was an appetite for doing things and learning things. I don't think it's a coincidence that you can't pick up your phone when your hands are covered in dough or clay, or busy weaving.

*

Next – and this may be where you're a bit different from me and are happy to live with more spontaneity (and not be the 'fun sponge' as my children sometimes call me) – for me, organisation is central to looking after myself. It's about having regular time cordoned off to catch up and/ or reflect on the big things (Sunday evenings work best for me); it's about having a strong to-do list system; and, most of all, about putting my energy into planning ahead rather than playing catch-up. In the end I spend the same amount of energy, whether I'm planning in advance or scrambling to sort something out at the last moment, so better the former, I think – and it is certainly less annoying for the people you have to lean on at the last minute due to being disorganised. Being 'a planner' makes me feel like a bit of a loser (my kids also tease me about my love for the label-maker), but life without organisation is hard work. It goes better if, for example, I spend time stocking up on a healthy lunch and snacks rather than rushing out to get a sandwich at 4 p.m. when only the nasty ones are left. It goes better if I spend time calmly planning work outfits in advance rather than sitting on my bed in the morning surrounded by clothes but with nothing that goes together. So I made a conscious decision a while back to place my energy into planning – my diary, my outfits, my food, my exercise sessions – not scrambling. I am embarrassed to admit that I am mildly obsessed with organisation (more on this later) – which is probably why my handbag designs are full of labelled pockets and internal compartments.

It's also, probably, why I like running a company – an 'organisation'.

Ironically, relaxing is something that falls into this category of organisation as it works better if I build this protected time – or 'stepping stones' – into my diary. I'm not sure why I think of them as stepping stones but perhaps it's because life sometimes feels a bit like stepping into a fast-flowing river, and I need to plan some breaks in the middle to help me cross safely to the other side. Stepping stones give me something good to look forward to, and even just knowing they're ahead makes the busy times more manageable. For example, when the children were younger, an au pair provided me with some crucial time on a Saturday morning. Nine times out of ten I would get up anyway, because I wanted to, but just knowing I didn't have to made a big difference. If I could spend another few minutes on a Saturday morning lying in bed and listening to our lovely au pair clunking around putting cereal in a bowl and the children playing dinosaurs, that was golden. I started my weekend feeling happy and on top rather than burdened and resentful. I know an au pair isn't an option for everyone. It worked for me but for someone else it could be a friend or a neighbour's teenage child or their mother.

Nowadays, if I look at my week and it's back-to-back, what gets me through might be planning in a gym session, or a glass of wine with some friends, or an hour off with a box set. That can get me through to the weekend, when I like doing nothing at all, apart from hanging out at home with my family, with no plans. If I'm doing anything, I want it to be with really close friends, kitchen table, no need to dress up, no make-up. That's my real 'off '. A commitment-free weekend is a perfect stepping stone, an opportunity to take a breath. I can catch up with the kids, do the maintenance jobs like getting my hair cut, go for a walk, sort whatever I didn't get to from the week before and plan for the week ahead. I'm conflicted because I both enjoy my weekend reflection time and also slightly resent that I'm having to do all that sorting and admin and work in my 'time off'. But ultimately, if I don't have that space to plan ahead, I start the next week already feeling like I'm drowning and that's no fun. My husband is completely different from me. He is fine on five hours' sleep. He can sleep on planes. He can drink four glasses of wine, go to bed at two in the morning and feel OK the next day. He finds socialising relaxing and likes nothing better than being around a table full of people at the weekend – as guest or host. But he has had to sacrifice that somewhat (he would say completely) because I just can't do that at the weekends and still function at pace during the week. I need the weekends to recuperate and recharge and recover. We tried it his way for a bit – I thought, *Yes, sure, I can make this work* – but actually I couldn't. I couldn't manage a full-on week of work, and then go and be a sparkling guest at the weekends. I got tired and sick and run-down.

And it didn't leave me any time to sort the birthday presents, and the thank-you letters, and the children needing to be here or there, or to catch up properly with them, or to reflect on the week just gone and plan for the next one. So, after a lot of talking around the subject, he made his peace with the fact that our weekends can't always be what he wants. It's tough on him, and it makes me feel bad, but the alternative is just unsustainable for me. At the sleep lecture I attended, Professor Foster said that people do have different sleep needs. I suppose I drew the short straw, but however hard I try, I can't find a way round my need for sleep. I often think about how much more I could achieve if only I needed less.

Stepping stones is a concept that works for me longer-term as well. If I look at my year and there are three months with no respite in them, I start to feel depleted and a bit resentful and I can go into victim mode. This has been something I am sure we have all suffered from during the pandemic. In more normal times, I would try and take the time to map things out in advance. That might mean a weekend away somewhere, but actually, if I'm doing a lot of travelling for work, then more travel could be exactly what I don't need. So it might instead mean a trip to the theatre, or gathering the family for a Sunday lunch, or supper with close friends: something that is going to nourish me and replenish me and allow me to come back to my life feeling positive and on top of my game.

Of course, the ultimate stepping stone is a holiday, and there are two types that work for me. Sometimes the most refreshing holidays are the real travelling ones with jam-packed itineraries that distract me from anything other than what I am doing that day, or the ones with a houseful of friends and kids, where I really let my hair down and get to the stage where I don't care if the office burns down! But there are times when I just need a bit of time 'off' on holiday, rather than being 'on' on holiday. Either way, I think the best holidays are three days or three weeks. Three days is short enough to park the phone and completely give in, and three weeks (which I rarely get) tends to go like this: week one is wind-down, week two is fun, and week three is when I stop caring and do a really deep recharge and the big thinking. If I get a holiday right – exercise, sleep, time outside or just undemanding fun with real friends – I come home rebalanced and ready to climb the next mountain. Although on arrival it can sometimes take me a couple of days to wind down. The adrenalin that was keeping me going has stopped and I'm left feeling scratchy and even a bit blue. But it soon passes.

Finally, when I'm completely fried with work and travel and home and when I just feel like I have nothing left to give, it is easy to overlook the deep satisfaction to be gained from helping someone else. It's a win-win. Not only is 'doing for others' the right thing to do, but it is also nourishing and rewarding: it meets a basic need, and I think that you can't be properly balanced and happy without it. It can be as simple as doing something kind for a mum at the children's school who is struggling; giving a leg-up to someone trying to break into your industry; or using your own platform to raise funds or awareness. Big things can be an amazing rush but the small private things – as simple as giving someone who needs it a boost – are often even more deeply satisfying. There is no barrier to entry, no financial cost, and nothing gets me out of an exhausted self-pity slump more quickly.

*

I worry that my jumble of thoughts above might sound like I'm complaining, but I promise that I'm not. The acupuncturist was right. I chose all of the elements in my life that keep me busy, and I keep choosing them – so I needed to find strategies to make all of them fit together and work. These are the strategies that keep me from getting overwhelmed, 'doing dominoes' or burning out. I always liken burnout to sunburn: by the time you realise you're in danger, it's too late – it's already happened. So you have to learn how much exposure you can take, learn to recognise your tell-tale warning signs, and make sure you cover up accordingly. Exercising, eating healthily, getting enough sleep and organising myself so I have breaks planned ahead are my sunscreen. If I get those right, I can put my face in the sun and enjoy its warmth. If I don't, I am taking my chances.

4

Fear and Excitement Are the Same Emotion

I didn't thrive at school, but I really loved music. I did a lot of singing and took it really quite seriously, to the extent that I was considering it as a career. One year, when I was about thirteen, I was entered into the school music competition. I remember feeling super-nervous but also quite excited about it.

The school hall was packed with people. It wasn't quite the whole school, but my parents were there, of course, and Sister Angela and the other teachers, and all my friends. A big chunk of everyone in the world whose opinion mattered to me was in the audience.

Walking out from the wings onto the stage was a big, scary moment for me. There was clapping and then silence. I remember my music teacher playing the introduction on the piano and I remember the moment I was meant to come in, but I didn't come in. My music teacher stopped playing and said, 'Don't worry, we'll do it again.'

It was one of the most mortifying experiences of my life. I absolutely, viscerally understood what it meant to want the ground to swallow you up. I wanted to sink into the boards of the stage and not have to be conscious any more.

I don't remember what happened afterwards. I don't think anyone said, 'Don't worry, it's fine, these things happen.' I think it was awful and embarrassing for everyone.

That was the last time I sang in public. I still sang privately in my lessons and in choirs. But drying up so publicly really knocked me and I couldn't come back from it. After a while my general confidence bounced back but I wouldn't sing, or speak, in front of an audience.

In fact, if I ever tried to, I couldn't. If I stood up to sing a solo or to speak in front of a group of people, I would start to become overly aware of my breathing. I would feel I had to get just one more breath in before I started. Just one more breath. By the time I managed to get going, I was always late, and/or gulping for air.

While my company was still just two, three and four people, I could manage the situation. But as it grew, I needed to be able to stand up and talk to bigger groups: sometimes eighty or a hundred people in a room. It was a basic part of my job, but I couldn't do it properly. I wanted to be motivating my team, and giving them confidence in me and in the company, but that was difficult when I was struggling to breathe from fear. I dreaded it every time.

As life got busier and more stressful, the situation got worse. Every time I had to do a scary meeting, or give a scary presentation, or got nervous about anything (which was often), I found myself gasping, desperate to get to the top of my breath. I was hyperventilating.

I felt silly and embarrassed about it. I read up on it, and the best advice I could find was to breathe into a paper bag. But that really wasn't practical. Where was I supposed to go with my paper bag before a meeting? So I was just living with it, ashamed and also annoyed, knowing it was holding me back. By this time I had got to a point in my career when I was being invited to give talks to various groups – women in business, entrepreneurs, school students, industry groups – and even though I had things I wanted to say and thoughts I wanted to share, I was turning them all down. My fears were getting in my way.

In the run-up to the launch of one particular, very public, project, when I knew I was going to have to stand up in front of a thousand people – literally, I just had to say seven lines – I started waking up gasping for air in the middle of the night.

I said to a friend, 'This is stupid. It's just talking. And we all know I can talk. So why can't I do it with an audience? There's no difference. It's still just breath going in and breath coming out.' And my friend very gently and kindly suggested someone I should see about it. 'He does this thing called NLP, neuro-linguistic programming. It's a sort of therapy-treatment-chat.'

So I went to see William Scott-Masson: ex-army officer, professional actor and NLP practitioner. And I decided that I was going to embrace it, whatever this therapy-treatment-chat was. I wanted to fix this, and I was going to be open to whatever he had to say, listen hard and go *all in*.

It took just one session. In one session, William reversed the problem that had undermined me and limited me for probably twenty-five years, and made a major impact on my life. His approach was to take me through the original trauma – in my case, the singing competition – in lots of different ways. He asked me to replay it in my mind with a Mickey Mouse voice instead of a human voice. He asked me to see it in black and white. He asked me to think it through in reverse. He took me through all kinds of visualisation and audio exercises, with the aim of scrubbing the existing version of 'the incident' from the brain and replacing it with something that had less power over me. As I write it, it sounds fanciful, but I can only tell you that it worked.

William also revealed to me a powerful idea that had never occurred to me but which I understood immediately to be true: he told me that fear and excitement are actually the same emotion. They are the same thing, they make you feel the same way, and you can decide: are you feeling fear or are you feeling excitement? So, in fact, when I'm going to stand up and make a speech, I'm frightened – because it might go wrong and that would be bad. But I am also excited – because it might go well and that would be great. I like a platform – and who doesn't? – to talk to other people about what I think is interesting.

It was like a penny dropping for me. It made total sense. As an entrepreneur, I'm frightened all the time: frightened I'm hiring the wrong person, or frightened that the idea won't translate into reality, or frightened the papers for the lease won't get signed. There are a thousand frightening things and you learn to live with that knot-in-the-pit-of-the-stomach feeling. And yet . . . I keep going because it is also exciting the whole time.

The power of the brain is phenomenal. William flipped a switch. Fear is just excitement.

The final thing William did – all in this one session – was to discuss the little voice in my head, the little gremlin on my shoulder that whispers in my ear, 'Don't mess up, don't mess up, don't mess up.' I had seen it as a terrible affliction and weakness. William explained that it was in fact a gift. The voice, the gremlin, was there to protect me. But he pointed out that actually, looking back on my life, I had not messed up very often. So I didn't need to silence the voice or kill the gremlin, I just needed to turn down the volume a bit. To learn to trust myself.

After my session with William, I forced myself to accept the next invitation that came along, from a group of feisty, bright, high-achieving women who called themselves the Kit Cat Club. It would be me, talking for an hour, to a group of women I highly rated. They wanted to hear about subjects I knew a lot about: my background, the challenges of starting a business, the future of the luxury industry post-financial crash, and my biggest campaigns. For a normal person it would have been a walk in the park, no preparation needed. For me it felt like the biggest personal test of my life. I was absolutely terrified. But I decided it was a mountain I had to climb, a flag I had to plant, because if I didn't I would be forever holding back on things that I really wanted to do.

Before I left the house that evening, I took a beta blocker. That's what it had come to by then. As I was leaving, my hands were shaking and I remember thinking, *Maybe I should have a shot of vodka?* In the cab on the way there I mainlined Rescue Remedy. I felt trapped in the car and just desperately wanted to escape. I thought I might actually get the driver to stop the car and run away. But I made it to the venue, where my sister was waiting for me. She knew what this was for me, and she took me to the bathroom and told me to calm down and reminded me to breathe.

I did it. It went well. There was even a moment when I was quite enjoying it. And afterwards, I got dozens of lovely letters from people who had been there, saying how much they had enjoyed it and how much it had resonated with them. One of them even said it was the best talk she had been to. That feels a bit boastful to say but I am saying it anyway because I want to make the point that sometimes the things you are most scared of are not only the things that excite you the most, they are actually the things you could be good at. When I speak, it gives me a voice. I have things to say, and mostly people respond, and things happen. That fear you feel is also excitement, and both of those feelings mean that whatever it is, it is meaningful to you.

It took a few more sessions to get to the point where I could do it without beta blockers, but luckily I never had to resort to the vodka shot, which would obviously not have helped. If I have a big speech to deliver, I will go back to William and run through it with him. Mostly he just tells me it's OK and laughs at the right moments, but he also gives me really thoughtful feedback, which in turn gives me the confidence to go a bit deeper into a bit that's meant to be humorous, or be a little more serious where that is what is needed. The person who does that for you doesn't need to be a professional. It could be a friend, or your husband (although my own husband, who writes really good speeches himself, is not always helpful when it comes to mine, which is probably a classic case of husbanditis). But NLP scrubbed the trauma for me.

I also picked up a couple of other tricks as I went along. I was about to give a speech at a dinner once and I was feeling wobbly. I admitted my fears to the actress sitting next to me. She said, 'Breathe in and count to ten. Now breathe out, and as you do, imagine little gold sparkles all around your body, from the top of your head all the way down to your toes.' I think because it distracts my mind and allows me to completely focus on my breath and my body, it absolutely works.

A dear friend also coached me in visualisation. She said that before a speaking engagement, you should imagine yourself standing there, in the room you are going to be speaking in. See everything in that room. Be specific: the podium, the curtains, which skirt you are wearing, which shoes. Look at the audience and clock them. Take a breath. Now you are going to look them in the eye and tell them your story. And at the end you are going to smile and they are going to clap. She said it was important to go through the whole thing in your head, because it opens up your neural pathways. Athletes use this method in their training, apparently – it's like a supercharged practice. They imagine themselves running the whole race, the roar of the crowd, breaking the tape, the feeling of winning, looking up and seeing their time.

They log the whole thing in their brain and it actually helps it to happen. It sounds far-fetched but it works.

The Kit Cat Club speech was a scaling-the-mountain moment for me. Since then I have made lots of speeches, given talks, addressed various audiences, big and small. And I would almost say that I now quite like public speaking. Do I still find it frightening? Yes. Do I find it a challenge every time? Yes. Do I still prepare very very hard to make sure I know exactly what I'm going to say? Yes. But I genuinely try to think of that as excitement, not fear. It was a lesson to me that you can crack your deepest fears if you really want to.

For me, self-confidence is like a muscle. If you make yourself use it, maybe even beyond what is really comfortable, it gets stronger. Even if it's tiny weights at first. Overcoming fear, like building up your muscles, can give you a real buzz. To switch the metaphor, once you have climbed one mountain, you find other mountains to conquer. Having scaled one, you realise perhaps you could tackle the next one, maybe a slightly higher one. Opportunities present themselves that maybe previously you would have turned down, and you're able to take them up. *That's a bit too scary* becomes *That's quite exciting, and I'll find my way.*

After the success of my NLP sessions, I started to actively put myself in situations that scared me because

I realised that the fear/excitement place was where I did some of my best work.

It was one of the factors that led to the launch of our London Fashion Week shows in 2012. Apparently, no accessories brand had had a catwalk show at London Fashion Week before. I had to beg for the slot, and then felt enormous pressure to justify the faith that had been shown in me and earn the approval of the fashion pack in attendance. Every single one of those shows properly terrified me – not least when my front row line-up included Anna Wintour, who (in her sunglasses, of course) asked for a 'walk-through' before the show. It was only about a week after each one was over that I could enjoy them. Only once the adrenalin had disappeared and my jaw had unclenched could I play back the film of the event and say, 'Actually, that was a beautiful thing.' But as time went on, and I had more and more events under my belt, I was able to say to myself, when the fear became overwhelming: *Anya, you will somehow pull it off. Take a breath. Trust yourself. It will be OK.*

That embrace of fear/excitement is also what has led me to accept some lovely but quite grown-up trusteeships over the last ten years, despite sometimes having a bad case of impostor syndrome.

In 2010, I was asked to become a Business Ambassador for the UK. The role entailed promoting business and banging the drum for UK export, and it was going to involve going out and making speeches to the British Chambers of Commerce and other such august bodies, and going to British embassies around the world to talk about trade. I nearly turned it down. I had turned down similar things in the past because I hadn't been sure I was ready. But I pushed myself to say yes. When I attended my first meeting, at 10 Downing Street no less, I looked around the table and felt inexperienced. I was probably the youngest and undoubtedly the least distinguished person in the room. But I will always be grateful to Digby Jones, Baron Jones of Birmingham, who was very kind to me. I have found that, in general, people are kind and generous if you step up and admit you're a bit nervous. He could see I was feeling like the newbie and he advised me, 'Just think of one thing you can do that will make a difference, and do that really really well.' It was great advice. I was there, I had been asked to be there, so I had to think about what I could contribute. And after giving it a lot of thought I decided that what I could do, and what I was really excited about, was entrepreneurship. I was never going to negotiate an international trade deal between Rolls-Royce and Boeing, but I could talk forever about the fun of the journey, the independence, the game of chess you play every day, and how crucial small businesses are as the engine of the economy.

So, with sponsorship from HSBC and help from a team at Number 10, I set up something that ran for a few years called the Entrepreneurs Exchange. At six o'clock on a chosen Tuesday, forty speakers gave talks in town halls across the country, free, for entrepreneurs to come along and listen to. I was very grateful to some really great people who agreed to travel far and wide to do these talks: Charles Dunstone from Carphone Warehouse, Julian Metcalfe from Pret A Manger, Natalie Massenet from Net-a-Porter, Fairfax Hall from Sipsmith, Justine Roberts from Mumsnet and John Vincent from Leon, amongst others.

Ideally everyone would have an inspiring and committed mentor when setting up and scaling a business, because I truly believe it is mentors, not money, that people need most when they're starting out: mentorship, and inspiration, and the stories of people who have hit the same brick wall but found a way through it, over it or round it. I hoped that this kind of group mentoring was the next best thing.

What I learnt from this experience was that probably almost everyone at that 10 Downing Street meeting had had similar feelings to mine at different times in their careers. They would all probably admit that they didn't know what they were talking about half the time. I don't mean that to sound rude or as if they didn't deserve to be there. They were lovely, kind, supportive and very able people. I just mean: if you think you are the only one in the room feeling like you don't belong, you are almost certainly wrong. I think these people have learnt to sit with those feelings and tolerate them and push through them. Instead of thinking *What am I doing here?* they're thinking *What can I do here?* They are working out what they can contribute.

And I did make a speech to several hundred people at the British Chambers of Commerce. If you had told me, back when I was hyperventilating in the back of a car at the thought of talking to eighty people at the Kit Cat Club, that I would stand up and give a speech to an auditorium packed with hundreds of people, I would have said, 'Absolutely not.' I would have said, 'You could offer me twenty million pounds – and, believe me, that would be really helpful in so many ways – but there is still no way I could do it.'

Buying back my business in 2019, having sold part of it in 2012, was probably one of the scariest and hardest things I have ever done. But it was also the most exciting. I know that if I hadn't trained on all the mountains that came before, I would never have made it to the top of this one. It took all my fight, all my grit, all the self-belief that I could muster.

The more mountains you climb, the more confident you become. And the more confident you become, the bigger the mountain you can tackle next. If you keep proving yourself, you learn to trust yourself – and you realise that often the only limitations are the barriers you impose on yourself. So it is important to try to break those barriers down. Getting over the fear of public speaking was a huge milestone for me, but more importantly it showed me that you can do almost anything if you're determined enough. 'You can do anything if you are determined enough' used to be a little catchphrase between my sister and me when we were younger. I actually remember engraving it onto a bracelet for her eighteenth birthday. Now I know that it's true.

Of course, there are many things I'm still too scared to tackle. There are plenty of fears I haven't yet conquered. I would love to be the kind of person who could run a marathon, for example, but the thought seems impossible to me and I just cannot imagine ever achieving that. But that's OK. It's OK to still have mountains to climb. It's OK to self-limit. And, who knows, maybe at some point I will decide I am ready. Never say never. (Although I'm laughing as I write this: marathons and me really are a never.)

Everyone has self-doubt, even people at the top of their game. Everyone is still sometimes thinking: *Could I? Should I?* Self-doubt is completely normal. It is also of limited value. It doesn't really get you anywhere. You are usually better just to push on.

Self-talk is something that really helps me. Recently I had a big interview to do for an important project and

I knew I was going to need to have a lot of facts at my fingertips, which I was finding scary. My breathing was starting to go, so to psych myself up (I am a bit embarrassed to admit this) I literally stood up in my office and said out loud: 'Anya, you're a grown woman. You've brought up five children for f**k's sake. Get a grip, you can do this.' The interview went absolutely fine.

Sometimes I will be sitting at dinner with a group of people and I'll look around the table and my inner voice – the gremlin on my shoulder – will say, *Everyone else here is funnier and cleverer and more beautiful than me.* I feel pathetic admitting this but it's true. I still have to consciously turn that inner voice down and find another voice that says, *Actually, Anya, get a grip.*

I have always kept lovely emails and notes and if I ever need a boost, I look over those as a nice reminder of things that have gone well. If my inner voice is pulling me down, having a delve in that special inbox pulls me back up again. If I can't physically get the notes out, I go back in my head to a time or a situation when I did feel comfortable and strong. I try to really go back to the moment and to recreate how it felt. Surrounding myself with certain people can also help. We all know there are people (maybe where the chemistry is just right) who boost us and make us feel like we are the best version of ourselves, and there are people who, though they might be our friends, just don't. Those friends bring other things to the table and are valuable in different ways but sometimes it gives a useful lift to be with the more bolstering friends.

And, having turned fifty, I keep having to remind myself that within my industry I am an 'elder' now. I don't feel senior but I know that I am, which brings with it a certain responsibility. Like everybody at my age, I think, half the time I'm still making it up as I go along. Just because people think I know what I'm talking about, it doesn't mean that I do. But I suppose I do think I'm at least quite good by now at making it up as I go along. And I am also quite good, I hope, at bringing people with me without pretending to know all the answers. Of course there are moments when people need 100 per cent confident leadership but there are also times when it's OK to lead by saying, 'You know what, I don't quite know, it could go wrong, but let's try this.' It's OK to be honest and a bit vulnerable.

I have realised that fear is not something to be avoided. Once I'd accepted that fear and excitement are two halves of the same coin, fear became something to seek out, to embrace. For me, at least, the fear is a necessary part of summoning the adrenalin to get something done to the best of my ability.

Fear equals excitement, but also 'things lead to things'. When you drop a pebble into a puddle you create ripples. Similarly, when you do something, you create a reaction. You can't necessarily imagine, in advance, what that reaction will be. But one dropped pebble can create momentum and open up big opportunities. When you tackle something scary or difficult, you always get something back. Throw energy at things, and you will get energy back.

Think about something good that has happened in your life and go back and trace how that came about and all the actions you took that led to that result. I often think back to the time, about twenty years ago now, when I was doing a project for British Airways, designing their amenity kits (the little washbags with a mini-toothbrush and so on inside) for First Class and Concorde. It was a fun project but it grew beyond its original scope, and so I needed to increase the capacity of my creative team. I was wandering through the Conran Shop in London – a place where I always find inspiration – and I noticed two men brilliantly 'visually merchandising' products in the way that only Conran does, which makes me want to buy everything. I thought perhaps I should approach them and ask whether they were freelance and might be interested in helping me out. But it felt too brazen and anyway it was late, the shop was about to close, and I needed to get going. So I carried on walking. At the last moment, with the sales assistant politely trying to usher me out so she could lock up, I stopped, turned back and tapped one of them on the shoulder, pressing my business card into his hand in a slightly embarrassed way. A few days later, Matt and Bevan, as I discovered they were called, got in touch. They came on board as external creatives on the British Airways project and we continued to work together over the next few years until eventually they both joined the business in-house. We ended up collaborating, for fifteen years, on many of the creative projects I am most proud of. Had I not headed to Conran for inspiration, and had I not forced myself to tap Matt, or perhaps Bevan, on the shoulder – had I just hurried along as I was meant to – the subsequent chain of events and some of those projects might never have happened. That shoulder tap was the pebble that caused the ripples. Always drop the pebble – always *do things*.

So take a tiny risk. Gain some confidence, then take a slightly bigger risk. Dare yourself. Do things. Push yourself a little bit. Build your trust in yourself. Not to the extent that you feel a failure, because there's no merit in that. Just a bit beyond comfortable. You will be amazed how far you can go.

5

Tight Ropes and Triangles of Pain

I started my own business straight from school, aged eighteen, in 1987. This was Margaret Thatcher's Britain, and my family was already so full of entrepreneurs that we used to joke that Christmas lunch felt like a board meeting, with everyone delivering their end-of-year results over the stuffing and roast potatoes, so starting my own business felt like a very natural thing to do. I also already knew that, though I might have been pretty unexceptional at school, I had an eye for design and I knew how to sell.

The beginning was very simple. I went to Italy, spotted a cool bag I thought I could sell back home, and convinced a factory I found in the *Pagine Gialle* (Yellow Pages) to make up samples. I took the samples back to the UK and, through a friend of a friend's stepmother who worked there, persuaded *Harpers & Queen* to sell my bags as their monthly offer. I sold nearly 500 bags, made £7,000 profit and suddenly further education seemed much less interesting.

There have been many ups and downs, much tacking and morphing, as we have responded to a changing world in the thirty-plus years since then. But there have also been constants. I initially thought I would learn to make my own pieces but quickly realised that a) I would do it very badly, and b) it wouldn't be a good use of my time. I toyed with the idea of having my own factory but, again, decided that running a factory wasn't my skill set: I needed to stick to what I did best, which was designing, selling, marketing and running a business. In 1992 a friend I had met in Florence, Annabel, joined me as production manager and my first proper employee. I couldn't afford a proper desk so her desk was made from two strips of melamine that collapsed if she typed too hard, which luckily made us laugh. In 1993, aged twenty-four, having built up a bit of a wholesale business selling handbags out of my suitcase into department stores, I tiptoed into retail. I moved the office out of my home, opened my first 'store' – a store-cum-office/design studio/dispatch centre on Walton Street in Knightsbridge, London – and managed to persuade a young graduate called Lisa to join us to manage sales. Lisa had a business degree, experience at Christian Lacroix in Paris and spoke five languages. We did the maths and worked out that we could afford her if she sold one bag a week. I am still not sure if that says more about our margins or what I was paying her in those days, but we worked together cheek by jowl for the next twenty-five years until she married and moved to Scotland. I owe so much to Annabel and Lisa (and all the fantastic women who took a chance on me right at the beginning), and the shared experiences and stories of those days still make us weep with laughter when we meet up. The store was on the first floor, which was unconventional, but a lot of amazing people climbed that rickety little staircase to come and see us in our little atelier. It was great to finally meet our customers and get their direct feedback; and it was useful to be able to design a physical world around the product, which gave it a context but also gave us a blueprint to replicate as we opened more stores around the world.

The wholesale business grew and we started exporting to stores like Bergdorf Goodman and Barneys in New York, Isetan in Tokyo, Joyce in Hong Kong and Singapore, Bon Marché in Paris, and so on. A year after opening on Walton Street, in 1994, I opened a franchise in Hong Kong, simply because Elizabeth Gouw, a Hong Kong Chinese graduate of the London School of Economics, asked if I would be interested in opening a store with her: she kept being asked by her friends to bring the bags back home. I thought, *Why not?* So that was the start of our franchise model, which was a great way to expand without capital expenditure. I'll never forget going to Hong Kong for the first time to see the store. I had insisted on it not being in a mall as it felt so alien and un-European, only to realise my naivety as I experienced the heat and humidity navigating my way to see the tiny store on On Lan Street. Our second store in Hong Kong was in an air-conditioned mall. I also vividly remember arriving in Hong Kong for the opening and driving by the store the night before, and being astounded by the scaffolding made of bamboo.

My first big charity project, *Be A Bag* in 2001, was born out of a new digital printing technique that allowed us to make affordable one-off bespoke bags with customers' photographs printed on the outside. The *I'm Not A Plastic Bag* campaign, a passion project aimed at reducing the use of plastic bags, was 2007. Our first London Fashion Week show was in 2012, and 2018 saw us break away from staging shows for the fashion industry and move into experiential direct-to-consumer events. By 2015, we had fifty-eight stores in eleven countries including Japan, Malaysia, Singapore, Taiwan, China, Hong Kong and the United States, plus a bespoke workshop on Pont Street in London.

Meanwhile, in 2007, we had brought our first investors into the business: a very happy, collaborative experience with people who were and remain dear friends. Five years later, we sold part of the business, took in new investors and brought in our first external CEO. In 2019, supported by my wonderful new business partners the Marandi family and their fantastic operating partner Enrique, we bought the (not very healthy) business back again and spearheaded a shift in the business model from stores to digital.

What kind of person makes a good entrepreneur? I strongly believe that it's all about character traits and not much about school smarts. To run your own business you need conviction, passion and positivity (at least to the point of infectious enthusiasm and often to the point of obsession).

You need to be determined beyond sense – for many years we underwrote the business with our house, even with five children depending on us for a roof over their heads – and you need enough optimism that others will believe in it too. Even before you get as far as hiring staff, you need to be someone that other people want to work with because you will be dealing with customers and suppliers and landlords and contractors and you'll have to be able to persuade them to buy from you, sell for you, rent to you, prioritise you, follow you.

I think emotional intelligence and empathy are more important than book learning. A combination of both is the best, of course, but if you can only have one then have emotional intelligence, because the rest you can hire.

Throwing a huge amount of energy at things tends to make you a lot luckier. Passion and enthusiasm will carry you a long way. Entrepreneurs are often energetic to the point of seeming slapdash. They are the people who don't bother with the instructions and want to skip steps so they can just get on with things. At school I was always the girl who never did the tacking and wanted to get straight on to the sewing. (Yes, girls still did sewing classes in those days.)

In my experience, successful entrepreneurs are also often quite simple thinkers. I don't mean that in a derogatory sense and I definitely include myself in this category. They are people who don't over-intellectualise, don't over-complicate things, don't want to debate things. They don't want to read everything and cross-reference everything before they get going. They maybe tend to skim a bit and be a bit broad-brush. They are straightforward – perhaps even a little naive. They don't want to cross every 't' and dot every 'i' before they take a punt, they just want to get their feet wet, jump in and find a way.

Entrepreneurs need to be determined, dogged, hard-working, resilient. They need the ability to try something, fail, and try again. To lean into the problem rather than abandon it. I often think of this quote attributed to Albert Einstein: 'It's not that I'm so smart, it's just that I stay with problems longer.'

All of this helps to explain why there are so many dyslexic entrepreneurs – more on average than in the general population. If you are intelligent and energetic and ambitious but don't thrive in an academic environment, then starting your own business is a very attractive option. You don't have to struggle through getting degrees – you can just crack on. And if you have already had to overcome dyslexia in school, you probably have built up some of the grit and determination, and the level of comfort with going against the flow, that you are going to need.

I was sitting in a government meeting about 'promoting entrepreneurship' once and someone from the Department of Business, Innovation and Skills said, 'We are very excited – we have a new book full of advice for entrepreneurs.' And they heaved it onto the table. I laughed. 'That's a tome,' I said. 'They are never going to read it.' Most entrepreneurs will not take the time to read a huge book. They will read the two-page summary, then just get going based on instinct.

My point is: you don't need to be at the top of the class at school to do well in business.

Other than that, learn to touch-type, make sure you look people in the eye, spend some time in an office or a factory or hanging around a start-up, and it never does any harm to know your way around a balance sheet, a profit-and-loss account and a cash flow.

Most importantly, you need to be prepared to be challenged and uncomfortable and a bit scared most of the time. It's not for people who need their job to feel safe – although these days, what job does? And in fact, though the advice I share in this chapter may chime mostly with would-be or existing entrepreneurs, I hope that anyone who enjoys innovating, or building, or selling, or organising, or just making things happen – including people in 'real jobs' – will be able to take something from these pages.

*

So what do you need to get started in business? First, you need an idea. Do you have an idea for something people will pay for that you can buy or make and then sell for more than it cost you? If you do, then you have a potential business. If you don't, you don't. That is, fundamentally, what a business is. It's about making profit. Sometimes people get caught up in really wanting to make something but they haven't spent enough time working out if there is really a customer. Or they can't sell it at a price that people want to pay and which allows for a healthy margin. That can be great, as a hobby, but it is not a business. Unless you have that profit box ticked, it's not a business. It's as simple as that. Yes, it gets more complicated when you get into cash-flow forecasting and business plans and so on. But ultimately, you buy something, or you make something, and you sell it for more than it cost you. And within your costs you have to remember your own salary, and your rent, and your materials, and all your other costs. If you have all of that, then you have a business. You are an entrepreneur.

It doesn't have to be a Big Idea or even an Original Idea. It can just be doing something better than anyone else is currently doing it.

Second, you need to be prepared to be lonely. For years, my office was my kitchen table. I sat there on my own, day in, day out, while my friends were enjoying themselves at university. For a while my sister joined me and ran her company from my kitchen table too, which was great, because I love her to bits, but it also brought with it a few small moments of tension. My sister liked to arrive very early in the morning and she (I suppose understandably) held me responsible if I had used her milk for my breakfast when she had a client coming to visit. There was one time she ended up desperately spooning the milk out of my cereal bowl into her client's coffee cup. I remind her to this day that the client actually asked for another cup, so it can't have been that bad. LOL.

In amongst all the passion and enthusiasm, you need to be able to stay objective and keep focused on your goal. Nick Hurrell, when he was at Saatchi & Saatchi, once said to me – and it really struck a chord – that every time you leave the office at night, you should mentally fire yourself, and then in the morning you should come back as your successor. You should look at everything with fresh eyes, and ask, as if you were a brand-new CEO, *Right, what does this business need? What is the most effective thing I can do today? What is going to actually drive this business forward?* And then be ruthless about doing that, and not the other stuff piling up on your desk. It is easy to lose sight of the fundamentals, especially as the business grows and especially if you feel you're building a brand or making a community. When you're running a business, often your to-do list is 90 per cent things that don't make any difference to growing the business: the charity request, the client's daughter wanting an internship, the survey the landlord needs you to fill out. Instead, keep your energy for what actually drives the business forward. I sometimes think of it like trying to walk in a straight line towards your goal while being pelted from all sides with bottles; success is eventually getting there despite the bottles you've had lobbed at you along the way. I remember my father once saying that sometimes he put his whole in-tray in the bin so he could focus on the important things, knowing that anything important would come back to him. I could never bring myself to do that but he had a point.

Cash is king. Always. It's really always about having enough cash. I got an early lesson in this when I ordered too much stock and it sat under my kitchen table for a year and a half, and every time I sat down and ate my breakfast I kicked it. If you have cash, you can ride out most problems. If you don't, you can't and you will start making decisions for all the wrong reasons. I am writing this in the middle of the horrid pandemic and I suspect we will sadly soon see that it's the businesses that don't have cash that are the first to go. Cash is what you need to get through something like this. No one is thinking about profit – they just need to stay alive and then assess the damage on the other side.

However, Lord Young, one of my business heroes, once said 'There's nothing as dangerous as a young business with too much cash' – and I actually agree. It needs to be hard. You need to be tested at the beginning. The skills you develop when you're trying to make it work with not enough money are the skills you are always going to need to run the business. Which is lucky, because you can never rely on banks when you need them. I got going with a small loan from my parents (which I paid back – with interest!), and continued by using my home as collateral until the bank would allow it to be released.

Maybe even more than cash, entrepreneurs need mentors: experienced advisers who are ready to listen and offer advice. They can be invaluable to us driven but lonely people who are otherwise on our own with our problems, because often our problems are ones they've seen and solved before. And their company and their stories – the highs and the lows – can give us a lift when we have no one else to keep our spirits up and our outlook positive.

I am *enormously* lucky to have my father in this role (although he would never use the word 'mentor'). He is an exceptionally talented businessman and entrepreneur, having started his own business very young, and is one of the most clear-thinking, honourable and honest people I know. (So honest, in fact, that I often jokingly and affectionately call him my 'harshest critic'.) Being my parent as well as my 'mentor', his objectives are completely aligned with mine, and I feel less guilty about leaning on him than I would with someone not related to me. He takes my call at ten o'clock at night, listens to me for an hour, then calls me back in the morning saying, 'I've been thinking about this all night and I think this is what you should do.' I know he will always be brutally honest with me, and that he cares about me with no agenda of his own. 'Things lead to things', one of the principles by which I now run my business and my life, is something he says often, and, in tribute to him, was very nearly the title of this book. He gives me a tough act to follow with my own children.

Clearly I have been extremely lucky, but look around. Do you have an aunt, a godmother, a friend, a friend of a friend, or even a local retired businessperson who has some time? Anyone who will act as a sounding board, is prepared to be leant on a bit and will help you to believe in yourself. And when you can, pay it forward and do it for someone else.

*

When you set up your business, there will be that exciting day when you get your first business cards. Actually, these days business cards are less important. So . . . there will be an exciting day when your website goes live. And as you establish the business, there will be other exciting days: when you get your first order, when your first invoice gets paid, when you first make a profit. But, honestly, many days are a struggle.

It's what I call the triangle of pain. You have to get your products made, you have to get them sold, and you have to get paid. And each one feels almost impossible at times.

Getting them made was probably the toughest piece for me in the beginning. The pain was that I didn't have big-volume orders. When I started out, I wanted to make tens and twenties of my designs, not hundreds or thousands. Plus, because I was a new business, my product had to be more exciting than anything else on the market, so it couldn't be simple. I was asking manufacturers to make me a very complicated product for very small runs. I had to find people who would work with me for those kinds of minimums. I can't count the number of times I said, 'Little acorns grow into big trees.' That was the phrase I said again and again and again, to leather suppliers and hardware suppliers, asking them to please believe in me. And then, of course, they would always deliver late because, being their smallest customer, I was at the bottom of the pile in terms of priorities.

Getting them sold was initially about persuading department stores to write orders: to believe in my product and to put their budget into me rather than into a brand that had a track record. And then, of course, once they did, I became scared that I wouldn't be able to deliver on time – which brought me back to getting them made. If I didn't deliver on time they would dock 25 per cent off the invoice at best, or at worst just cancel the order.

I'm sure that everyone who has started their own business has their own version of that. If it's a tech start-up then it's about persuading the most sought-after developers, who everyone wants a piece of, and who charge by the minute, to give their time to you and your product. And then using their time wisely to make your product the best and the first to market.

As I grew and learnt, I moved to smaller suppliers and gave them all my work, so that I would become an important customer to them and be more likely to get my deliveries on time. It was all about persuasion. I was persuading people to make my product, persuading people to take my product, persuading people to pay me on time.

I had thought I was starting a business to be a designer. But designing, which was what I thought I was passionate about, was about 10 per cent of what I was doing. The rest of the time I was trying to work out VAT invoices, trying to get the DHL delivery unstuck, explaining that the order was running late because the packaging hadn't arrived. What was required was granular execution.

At least, though, these were the things that were driving the business forward and the things I needed to focus on. I also found myself spending half a day changing the toner cartridge in the photocopier. (Working out why the printer wasn't printing, working out which was the correct toner, getting to the shop, getting home again only to realise it wasn't the right one, back to the shop again . . .) It had to be done but there wasn't much sense of achievement and more importantly it didn't move my business forward at all. You have to try to stay focused on what is going to make a difference to your business, which is hard when there is no one to delegate anything to.

At this stage – and actually at pretty much every stage in a business's life – things go wrong that you could not possibly have anticipated. In fact, this is mostly a state of normal, and navigating this becomes the fabric of any success.

Very early on, I designed a bag inspired by an old perfume bottle. It was a complicated design that opened up like an umbrella and it had a metal perfume-bottle lid that clicked shut in a very satisfying way. It took me ages to work out how to get it made, because I didn't want something generic, but I couldn't achieve the minimums to interest hardware suppliers, and I couldn't anyway have afforded the moulds. So I approached a jewellery designer who had a workshop in Hackney, in an old converted hospital. She made the moulds and she cast them, and then in the same building there was a plater who could plate them and a finisher who could polish them. I loved sitting with these craftspeople and learning from them. But I was selling to New York, and Hong Kong, and Japan, and we didn't lacquer the plating. We left it matt, just beautifully silver-plated. I hadn't counted on the humidity in Hong Kong. On the way over there, because the metal wasn't sealed with a lacquer, the humidity made the metal 'bloom', and by the time it reached the buyer, every single metal lid was black. I had to take them all back, credit the buyers, absorb the delivery costs and have them remade.

A lot of businesses don't make it through this triangle-of-pain phase. It's hard and it's sticky. There are often cash-flow problems. The excitement of the new business cards has worn off and the day-to-day is full of problems. The trick, I think, is just not to give up and to find another way and to be flexible with your business model. Listen to what the customer is telling you. Adapt. Passion and positivity and energy and sheer bloody-mindedness are what get you through. Running a business is about hitting every brick wall and finding a way over it, round it or through it. And through sometimes hurts, let me tell you. That's all it is, really, nearly every day.

*

It is a huge step in the life of a business when you can build yourself a team. I can't tell you what a difference it made in my case. Suddenly I had someone to say 'Good morning' to, and someone to plan the day with. Somehow the very act of verbalising it – 'OK, let's do these five things today' – and writing it down and focusing someone else on the end goal helped to make it happen. It was a form of visualisation, I see now. It gave a shape to the day. We felt heroic if we got through our list and terrible if we didn't.

It's easier once you start employing people, because you have people to help you. But it's also more responsibility and pressure. It's now your job to give your employees what they need to do their jobs well. When the chips are down, people are looking to you to make the right decisions. If the business fails, the people you employ are out of a job. You also become obsessed with finding talent, and hanging on to the talent you've found. There has barely been a moment since I started employing people that I wasn't terrified one of them would leave.

As an entrepreneur you will always spend a large proportion of your time dealing with people. Even before you are employing people, you will be dealing with suppliers and buyers and landlords. You are having to win people over, constantly. Once you are employing people, though, your people skills need to sharpen up.

You don't have to change the toner cartridge any more. But you do have to keep the person changing the toner cartridge happy and motivated (and working hard). In fact, as the business grows, making sure you have a happy workforce full of people who feel good about themselves, and know what they are doing, and don't waste energy on politics and negativity, and love coming to work every day – keeping your people functioning like a well-oiled machine – becomes your most important job. Businesses often work not because of a brilliant idea but because it is a decent idea, brilliantly executed. And that is about committed, invested and talented people. People who follow through and are loyal and will roll up their sleeves and go the extra mile. You have to learn how to recruit good people and learn how to hang on to them; learn to communicate your goals so that everyone understands them; and learn how to get the best out of people. You need to invest energy and love and emotion into maintaining your most important machine.

Employ people who can do the stuff you can't, and always employ people who are better than you. You don't need to be incredibly clever to start a business but the incredibly clever people are often the people I am desperate to hire to grow the business: to get into the detail of the forecasting, and the supply-chain management, and the digital marketing, and the contracts. I now have the most brilliant team of people who do things I couldn't begin to do. Obviously if you can do the big picture *and* the detail, that's the dream, but it's quite unusual to get all of that in one person.

More importantly, employ people with the right attitude. My ideal is to create a fluid, positive, diverse, creative culture where people are not defensive about their ideas. I try to avoid recruiting people who have not learnt how to offer criticism without causing offence, nor how to take criticism with grace. These people, however talented or clever, become people that everyone else has to work around. You can't have many of those in an organisation or it becomes unsustainable.

Ultimately I have realised that it works best when I recruit people I would want to have dinner with. Obviously they need to be brilliant and have the right skills and to have done the relevant work and come with the right references. Perhaps less obviously, I should also make it clear that 'people I want to have dinner with' does not equal 'people who are like me'. What I mean by the dinner test is that I ask myself: *Does this person have the right positive and collaborative approach? Do I want to spend time with them?* And as a result I am lucky enough to work with the most fantastic group of people. We have lots of ideas and we work incredibly hard to pull them off. Sometimes they succeed and sometimes they don't but we always have fun trying and we often have dinner together.

A diverse workforce is vital, both ethically and commercially, but my position on how to achieve this has changed. Most of my career has been in the era of 'equality for women in the workplace'. It has not been achieved yet – clearly – but until recently I was somewhat sceptical about the various efforts made, and used to say, 'I don't want to be put on a board just because I'm wearing a skirt.' I felt that progress was being made and would continue to be, naturally and organically, as women continued to deliver and prove their worth. I argued against quotas or other measures to 'force' change, as it seemed to me that they could undermine women.

My mind was changed when I sat on a panel to debate the subject at a bank in the City of London. I listened to women in finance talking about the advantage men had of being able to walk into a boardroom knowing that their fathers and grandfathers had done the same before them. It was straightforward for these young men to creatively visualise themselves in the same place, able and deserving. These same women talked of endless clubby talk about golf handicaps and cricket amongst the powerful people in the room. It made me realise that there actually is a place for forcing the issue along a bit, for focusing on hiring more women into senior roles, so that our daughters can see role models and join in the conversation. It is not done yet, but there has been progress.

Since the Black Lives Matter movement gained such momentum I have thought a lot about how the issues surrounding race in the workplace are not dissimilar to the issues around women in the workplace. In my organisation we have nearly always had a diverse workforce and a diverse management team, including BIPOC, female and gay people in the top jobs. This has not been something I have positively sought out: it has happened naturally, as I have looked for the right people for the job. I always used to say that I didn't notice colour, that I just noticed whether someone was kind, smart or talented. I was corrected, in the nicest possible way, by someone on my team, who pointed out that not noticing someone's colour was disrespectful. He was right, of course. And the truth is that I do notice colour in the same way that I notice that someone has red hair, blonde hair or freckles, but shortly after that I notice whether someone is funny, smart or talented, and that is what counts.

I realise, though, that it is not the same in all organisations, and we could be better even in my own organisation, for example in the imagery we use to advertise our products. There is a lot more work to do. Businesses need to consciously resist the temptation to hire 'people like them'. We need to realise we are hugely disadvantaged if we do not hire a workforce that represents our customers. We need to ensure a pipeline of good candidates. And we need, perhaps, to force the issue for a bit, to create more role models as we have done for women.

That is the uncomfortable bit, because it might mean taking on someone who perhaps is less confident than another candidate. But what do we do when candidates don't get the job because they aren't confident, and they aren't confident because they didn't get the job? I think it is for employers to crack this vicious circle.

Once you have recruited someone, of course, you will then be fully focused on how to keep them. That means you have to be someone people want to work with – it has to be fun and/or good for their CV – because if you are a small business you will be trying to put all your money back into growing the business. That often means you can't afford to pay your people the market rate they could command somewhere bigger and slicker and nor can you give them everything they might want, and might deserve, in terms of bonuses and promotions and options.

So you have to find a way to make them want to stay with you. You have to deploy your passion and energy and positivity so that they will love the journey and the excitement of building something, they will believe in the business, they will love working with the team. I have come to realise that maybe I worried more than I needed to about this. Very often, as much as the salary and benefits and progression, job satisfaction is about liking your team, and enjoying working together to build something. It's about: *Am I having fun? Am I proud of what I'm doing? Are we collectively making a difference? Are we reaching our goal?* When all is said and done, people sometimes value the cake-baking competitions and the crazy weekend in Tokyo when the project nearly fell apart as much as a salary rise.

I always try to do people's appraisals before they go on a big holiday. Because I know that holiday is often a time when people take stock. Doing the appraisal beforehand means I can try to remind them of everything they like about the job, make sure they know they are valued and allow them to get things off their chest. I want to make sure they go away knowing that they are appreciated and feeling that whatever is bugging them has been acknowledged and is being dealt with.

And say thank you. Thank you for staying late, thank you for getting us out of that hole, thank you for sticking with that and making that happen, thank you for organising the leaving party. It is so easy, and free – not to mention courteous and respectful – so say thank you. It is obvious and it is essential. And yet so many people don't do it.

If being able to afford to employ people is one major milestone, taking on investment is another. As with recruitment, my learning is that it is so important to choose the right partner, and as with recruitment, I suggest the dinner test. Choose people you really like.

You need investors who are supportive of and aligned with your vision. But the vision will never be the reality so you also need your partners to back you and trust you, and to think the way you do. Because the moment you get an investor, you are working for someone else. I have been extremely lucky with my investors but not everyone is so fortunate. That's why I often say an investor isn't a badge of honour or a sign that your business is all grown-up – it's actually a booby prize. It shows you can't do it on your own any more. And you're no longer calling all the shots, which is really tough for an entrepreneur.

As the business grows, and whether you take on investment or not, you stop playing your instrument and become the conductor of the orchestra. It's your job to keep everyone focused on the same goal, to help everyone work together, and to keep everyone excited and positive and doing great work. It's your job to constantly remind people: 'This is what we are going for.' It's your job to build a sense of community and loyalty and pride. It's your job to make people want to come into work and do their best: to make the orchestra sound good together.

My approach is to communicate, communicate, communicate. The more you can communicate the better. And the more honestly and authentically the better. Just be you. Be honest, take people with you on the journey, and make it their journey too.

People need a confident leader, and there are certainly moments when you have to say, 'This is what we're doing and I absolutely believe in it.' But I think it's OK sometimes to say you don't have all the answers. It's OK to say, 'This is where we want to go and I don't know exactly how we will get there, but we will find our way.' It's OK to say, 'This is what I think but I want to hear from you.' Or even, 'I'm sorry, I got that wrong.' You can be assertive and confident and at the same time admit to not having all the answers. I don't think you should be scared about being openly vulnerable. You can get more buy-in sometimes if people realise that it's hard for you too. The people I've been most impressed with, and most fired up to do well for, have been people who have been confident and inspiring but also honest, and who have allowed themselves to be vulnerable and open about their fears.

Set out the goals for the year, chunk them down, then every week keep communicating those messages, keep repeating the plan, keep reminding people what they are aiming for. Make sure everyone knows where they are going.

I always talk about 'tight ropes' – meaning that the links from one part of the organisation to another are solid, not floppy. It means that if you went into our store on Pont Street and met Penny or Roy, they would handle any situation in the same way as I would (if not better), because they know what we stand for, and hopefully they feel connected enough to head office and the objectives to go the extra mile. Tight ropes save a thousand words. But the person running a store in Tokyo is a long way, physically and metaphorically, from head office in Battersea. How can I connect with them and ensure the culture in the store in Tokyo is the one I would want? How can they connect with me and let me know what is important to them and their customers? We instituted a very simple system where every night, as well as the automatic figures we would get from all the stores, each store manager would write me a few sentences. *This is how the store was yesterday. It poured with rain, we had a problem because there was a burglary in the street which shut things down for a bit, but actually Mrs [name] came in. She didn't like this but she liked that.* It gave me a great flavour. And all those tiny micro-messages, which are very quick to read, meant I could go back saying, 'Good job', or 'I'm sorry, did that break, let me work on that.' It meant we had a connection, it meant they felt they knew me better. The tight rope system is vital. The moment you have a slack rope you get a slack result.

Celebrate the successes and mourn the losses. Ring the bell when it goes well, crack open a nice bottle when you've achieved something wonderful, be sad but resilient when you haven't.

Communication isn't just about words. It's about how you behave, every day. True, authentic behaviour is much more important than a mission statement or endless grand words.

For example, if I want a culture where people are prepared to throw out ideas knowing they won't be judged, and to listen to ideas without judging, I have to think really hard about how I behave. In a meeting, how do I make sure everyone is heard? How do I react when someone comes up with a bad idea? How do I say something that lets everyone know it's OK to have a bad idea as bad ideas often lead to good ideas? What do I do when someone says something a bit aggressive or criticises someone in an abrasive way? Do I let it go or can I say something to take the corners off it? How can I josh, smooth, deflect, to keep things light? How can I lead by example, laughing at my own bad ideas?

Have a company motto if you feel it will help amplify the message. But your behaviour, every day, and the people you hire, and their behaviour every day, are so much more powerful at conveying your message than any motto can be.

I'm also hugely focused on building a sense of community. Money is exciting, and profit is the aim and inextricable from running a successful business. But building a business is also about building a community. Creating amazing memories and doing beautiful things can be aligned with realising profit and growth. I don't think one has to be at the expense of another. In fact, they often support each other.

So we spend a lot of time celebrating birthdays, throwing baby showers, making shared memories and creating a sense of a work family. For me, it is critical to keep the ideas flowing, and to keep the energy working in a positive way rather than it being directed at sorting out resentments and blocking ideas. If I were ever considering buying a company, that is what my due diligence would focus on. I would have dinner with the management team and try to work out: are people defensive, are people abrasive, or is it a happy, jokey, fluid, supportive place where people aren't taking themselves too seriously? This is a valuable and yet invisible asset on a balance sheet that is often overlooked. Without this constructive team spirit I think it must be hard to be successful.

In business your first priority is to the business. The business employs and therefore feeds a lot of people, so that has to be the priority. You have to make the decisions, therefore, that are right for the business. That's number one. But then immediately following it is: *How can I make this decision as good as possible and as decent as possible? How do I find the kindest, fairest way to implement it? And how do I communicate it clearly and honestly: this is what, this is why, this is how?* Apart from it being the right thing to do, people can see through anything else.

I recently made the decision that we were going to close some of our stores. At the time of writing we have fourteen stores. At one point we had fifty-eight stores around the world and we were planning to grow to eighty and then one hundred and twenty. But a couple of years ago it became clear to me – even though emotionally it was a wrench – that cookie-cutter bricks and mortar was not the future and the business should become predominantly a digital one. The future business model had to involve using digital channels to communicate directly and deeply and quite personally with the consumer, with many fewer, more experiential stores. To become a more modern-shaped business, we needed to reduce our physical footprint fast. How do you do that respectfully, kindly and fairly? It is possible. You can do what is right for the business and be kind to people.

If you get the difficult times right they can even be strengthening. The financial crash in 2008 was a very scary moment for retail and I remember saying to everyone, 'We've got to bring our A-game now. We've got to fight like men with beards. It's going to be a tough time but we will get through it.' To try to save jobs, everyone agreed collectively to take a 10 per cent salary cut. Meanwhile, in response to the 'fight like men with beards' comment, the men in the company decided to have a beard-growing competition. We took 'before' and 'after' photos, like police mugshots. The Spaniard in the office had a full beard by five o'clock that afternoon, whereas the young British guy had a little tuft two months later. It was a hard time but we kept the business safe and it was very bonding – the 'temperature' of the AH community through this time was probably at an all-time high despite the challenges, and we had one of our more successful years, despite the lower turnover.

Facing our latest and biggest challenge, Covid-19, we have again had to focus on doing what is right – in this case for the health and safety of our people, as well as the health of our business – and then implementing that as kindly and fairly as possible, and communicating it as honestly and clearly as we can.

Through March and April of 2020 we had to make a series of very difficult decisions, very quickly. At first, before the lockdown, we were trying to find ways of keeping stores open safely, because we were trying to protect people's financial health as well as their physical health. We split the office into two and because our HQ had two floors we could reorganise our desks and become upstairs people and downstairs people. That was so that, if one person developed symptoms, we wouldn't have to send the whole organisation home to self-isolate. Everyone had a trial week working from home to make sure we would be ready if and when we had to close the office completely. We also divided the warehouses into two to de-risk our operations, and had to deal with the Italian factories closing down production.

And then it got to the stage where it didn't feel safe to keep the stores or the offices open and, almost overnight, we were doing the previously unthinkable and closing them all and putting them into hibernation. At the same time, we had wholesale customers who were needing to review their orders because department stores were closing. We then in turn had to work out how to reduce our orders for wholesale without hitting just one factory too hard. We didn't want to just push our problems up the supply chain. That felt like absolutely the wrong thing to do – making things OK for us by dumping our problems on someone else. So we reduced by a little bit across every supplier. All our events had to be postponed. Everyone in head office was working remotely and we had to communicate to staff in different countries where lockdowns were happening at different paces and in different ways. And, frankly, everyone was quite scared.

As everything was closing down, we also had to re-forecast all our numbers, work out where we could cut costs and try to find the fairest way to adjust salaries and furlough staff. We decided to keep all staff on £30,000 or below on their full salary. The directors all agreed to take a 15 per cent salary cut, and then we drew a straight line between the £30,000 salaries and the director salaries and people took a proportionate cut depending on where their salary fell on that line.

The people who were left unfurloughed – such as the digital teams and the directors (who had already taken a 15 per cent pay cut) – found themselves absorbing lots more work. Some of these directors were also juggling childcare with no help, trying to work from home while remote-schooling, or with a baby on one hip and a toddler on the other. And I know that if you have two tiny children at home all day that's a full-time job; there's no way you can work. So they were suddenly taking punches from all directions.

It was all very complicated and unfortunately I was ill myself with Covid for the first two weeks. (Not badly, thankfully.) But what I realised was that staying true to our values of kindness and fairness, even in crisis – especially in crisis – was key. I had to get the message clear and the tone right as the situation changed from day to day and from hour to hour. What struck me most forcefully was the need to communicate openly, regularly, honestly and personally. I did a lot of 'I don't know the answer to this, but I'm working on it' and 'I don't know how we're going to get through this, but we are going to find a way.'

Once we had our people safe and the business working in a new locked-down mode we turned our minds to what else we could do to help. We suggested to the staff we had furloughed that they volunteer their time for NHS Volunteers, or help in some other way if they felt they could. Some of them took on full-on nine-to-five days packing food boxes in village halls. We also put our design team and some of our suppliers to work producing 'holdsters' for ICU staff (at their request) so that they could carry their mobile phones and their pens and glasses around with them. And we organised the making and funding of washable gowns for healthcare professionals working at the Royal Marsden and St George's Hospitals. It made us all feel good to be able to do something other than just 'stay home' as instructed.

*

This chapter started with 'Who makes a good entrepreneur?' I want to finish not with *who* but with *why*. Why be an entrepreneur? First, because business is the engine of the economy. Entrepreneurs are the idiots who risk their houses to start a company. We should encourage these madmen who take risks to grow businesses and manufacture things and employ people and pay tax, because that's what pays for our hospitals and other vital public services, and allows us to look after not just the most vulnerable members of society but, as we discovered with Covid, every member of society. The pandemic has taught us, if we didn't already know, that we all need the state sometimes. Our healthcare workers are the true heroes of the pandemic. But the people who grow value and pay tax – in fact, all people who pay tax – are those who pay for these heroes.

But also, I can honestly say that having your own business is The Best Fun. The journey is fun. The struggle is fun. I realise now that the journey and the struggle are almost the best bit. I look back on the funny times and the stressful times – often they were the same times, somehow finding our way around and through, telling fibs, designing a whole collection in a weekend in a hotel room in Florence, pulling off a ridiculously complicated deadline against all the odds – and, truthfully, those memories are probably as rewarding as a big valuation and some money in the bank. Even if you don't achieve, the striving and the friendships and the people you work with are fun. They are a thrill. Every day feels like a combination of a game of chess and a lucky dip: you are plotting and strategising, and then dealing with whatever unexpected thing – maybe a huge new order, maybe a batch of ruined handbags – lands on your desk. You are pushing to make your vision happen. You are choosing your people and then watching them do amazing things. It's terrifying at times, but as we know that also means it's exciting. And if you are cut out for it, then even with its many drawbacks, it is – at least in my opinion – so much better working for yourself.

So, if you are reading this and wondering whether to do it, then my advice would be: do it. Expect failure. Expect difficulty. Take risks. Don't be scared to start again. And try to remember to enjoy the journey.

6

Creativity Will Eat Strategy for Breakfast

When I was about sixteen, a girl who had recently left the school came back to talk about her career in fashion. Afterwards I went back to my desk and I sketched a shop full of handbags, with me standing outside it and my name on the door. It was my way of saying to myself: *This is what I want to do.*

Two years later I had left school and was in Florence, the home of leather and the home of handbags, ostensibly doing a two-month language course to learn Italian, but what I was really doing was learning about the craftsmen, learning about the leather markets and the factories, and noticing that all the Italian girls were wearing a really cool drawstring duffel bag. Seven years after that – hard and sometimes lonely years building a wholesale business – I opened my first store, on Walton Street, and it was full of handbags and it had my name on it.

I didn't know it then, but the shop I drew aged sixteen was my first ever creative visualisation.

*

I love and admire proper craftspeople, who are obsessive about the way things are made: the kinds of people who work on my products, or people like my mother-in-law who always had some embroidery or papier-mâché project on the go. I love how they are always asking: *Couldn't we . . . ?* and *How about if we just . . . ?* and *Could I try . . . ?* I love the combination of artistry, technical nous and obsessive dedication: the way they work things out not just in their heads but also in their hands, by doing and making and trying different things. For me, craftspeople are the true creatives (and the true heroes of my business).

For a long time I didn't really appreciate my own creativity, or like to call myself creative, because I had no formal training in art or design. I wasn't the arty kid at school, particularly. I didn't do an art foundation course, I didn't go to fashion college, I didn't even do art GCSE and I'm really not very good at drawing. Everything I know about fashion, design and craftsmanship I have learnt on the job, from talking to people in the business, watching craftspeople and trying to make things work. But I came to realise that this was not a bad way to learn, especially for someone like me. I was always pretty impatient with classroom learning, probably because of being a little bit dyslexic. I also came to realise that creativity comes in many forms. I might not be great at drawing but I like to think I have good ideas – both in terms of having vision and in terms of then generating problem-solving ideas for how to make it happen. If my brain spits out ideas, it can be as useful as being good at drawing.

There is creativity everywhere. It is incredibly important in business and I don't just mean in the so-called creative industries, but in every business. If you are selling insurance (I am trying to think of a business that is not usually associated with creativity), you need to be creative about how you design your products, how you market them, what your sales patter is, how you engage your teams. You might be doing something quite humdrum that would never make it near a catwalk or an art gallery but if you package it differently, or find the right way to describe it, or make your team more excited about it, you can enthuse customers about it more and stand out from the competition.

Creativity is about solving problems and finding ways to do things well, and it is probably needed the most in the least 'creative' businesses.

I am proud of some of the creative ideas we have had in my own business over the years. No one really needs a new handbag, so it is important to me that each new design has a reason or tells a story or brings something fresh or beneficial into the world. But while I do love coming up with the initial concept, some of our most creative moments have been about solving the logistical problems, or the inevitable technical problems, or finding a way around one of the millions of roadblocks that every major project faces on its journey from idea to execution.

Our most fun and most successful projects have generally been the ones driven by passion rather than success. Obviously a successful outcome is the aim, but it is not my starting point and it is not what drives me. The starting point needs to be something I feel passionate about. It is when you are passionate about something that you will communicate most authentically about it, and be most successful at enthusing other people and creating momentum. Success is very often the by-product of passion.

Probably my biggest passion projects have been the *I'm Not A Plastic Bag* project, in 2007, and then, in 2020, the *I Am A Plastic Bag* project.

The idea for *I'm Not A Plastic Bag* came out of a brilliant little book called *Change the World for a Fiver*. Back in the mid-noughties, environmental issues were starting to tap on my shoulder and I am sure many others were feeling the same way. But I didn't know what I could do as an individual, and how I could make a difference. I had a light-bulb moment, however, when I was approached by Tim Ashton from the advertising agency Antidote, which was working with the social change movement We Are

What We Do (now known as Shift). We Are What We Do had published this little book of powerful ideas and number one of fifty said: 'Decline plastic bags wherever possible.' I realised we could use the platform of the 'it-bag' formula, which is one I don't particularly like but which is very potent, to encourage people to do one simple thing, which was to use fewer plastic bags.

Working in partnership with Antidote and We Are What We Do, we designed a canvas tote to highlight the overuse of plastic bags, with 'I'm NOT A Plastic Bag' stitched on the front. We priced it at £5 (to reflect the title of the book) and we launched it in the 'golden circle' of very fashion-forward stores – Colette in Paris, Dover Street Market in London, Isetan in Tokyo – and we put it on some very supportive celebrity arms. And then, as a second tier, I wanted to launch it with a supermarket, one of the major sources of the problem. We approached Sainsbury's, who were doing a big push to reduce their reliance on single-use plastics and were an incredible partner to work with. That combination of a cause people cared about, scarcity, a £5 price tag and worldwide distribution turned out to be a force to be reckoned with. The first run of 20,000 sold out in an hour; 80,000 people queued for it at Sainsbury's in the UK on its launch day. It went all around the world, getting bigger and bigger, with growing media and political interest. Each country had a different colour – London was brown, New York was navy – so some people even started collecting the set. People were camping out round the block outside Isetan, the department store in Tokyo, the day before the Japan launch.

It was not, however, a perfect, problem-free project. Firstly, I was no expert, I was just someone who wanted to use my fashion platform to encourage people to switch to reusable shopping bags from single-use plastic ones, and so I made mistakes. I had not understood that cotton is actually an environmentally controversial fabric. The cotton used in our bags was neither fair trade nor sustainable and we, quite fairly, took some criticism for that. It was annoying to get that wrong but as someone kindly said at the time, 'You have to crack a few eggs to make an omelette.'

The noise and the hype we created around the bag got louder and bigger than we had anticipated, and we were not equipped to deal with it. After Isetan, we launched at our own store in Ginza in Tokyo. People were getting so irritated with the length of the queue that the staff got nervous and insisted that I should be locked in the basement of the store for my own safety – which seemed ridiculous, frankly, but it gives you an idea of the mania for this bag. Finally, after Japan, we went on to launch in our store in the very chic Breeze Center in Taipei. People were queuing all around the outside of the mall to buy the bag, to the extent that the place could not safely open and there weren't enough safety barriers for the unexpectedly large crowd. Customers became angry, because they were not being allowed in. The people working inside the mall were also angry because they couldn't do any business. Then, when it did finally open, there was a surge and a stampede and we heard that thirty people ended up in hospital. Obviously we stopped the campaign at that point. There would have been one more launch but we cancelled it and made it into an online launch, which also promptly crashed the website.

We made mistakes, and they were amplified by the amount of attention the project was getting, not just in the fashion press but on a wider platform. But the aim of the project had been to raise awareness of the overuse of plastic, and awareness we certainly got. And, much more importantly, the conversations we contributed to made a difference: the British Retail Consortium, for example, estimated that in 2006, before the project, plastic bag consumption was 10.6 billion per year. By 2010, this had dropped to 6.1 billion. So back I went to my day job feeling that, despite the madness, we had achieved something.

However, more than a decade later, the problem was still far from over. Plastic bag consumption had declined dramatically but one phrase that I'd heard during the project in 2007 was still rattling around in my head: 'When you throw something away, there is no "away"'. The amount of plastic not being properly recycled and going into landfill is still shocking. I often think that if we all had to bury our own waste in our back gardens (whatever we couldn't recycle or compost) we would soon run out of space and we'd have to find alternatives to burying things in the ground. Today, the conversation has moved on to circularity – how can we reuse what is already out there rather than making more? There are 8 billion tons of plastic on the planet already. How can we keep it in circulation and out of landfill? I wanted not just to raise awareness this time, but also to demonstrate what was possible. As in 2007, it might not be perfect, but it would, I hoped, be progress.

And so we spent two years developing a beautiful fabric, which feels like a really luxurious cotton canvas but is actually made from recycled PET bottles. Because it behaves like a cotton canvas as well, it gets dirty, so we wanted to coat it to protect the fabric, but we wanted the coating to be recycled too. We managed to source a coating that was recycled PVB, which came from the laminate that is used between the layers of glass in a windscreen to stop it shattering. So each bag is made from thirty-two half-litre plastic bottles and coated in recycled windscreens. It's a really involved process: you recover the bottles, you smash them, you make them into pellets, you then melt the pellets, spin them into fibres and weave the fibres together to make the bag. It has a beautiful canvas feel on one side and the coating on the other. It is genuinely a work of modern craftsmanship, and we called it *I Am A Plastic Bag*. The project was actually my husband's idea, even though it pains me to admit it!

For London Fashion Week in February 2020, instead of having a show we closed our stores and filled them with 90,000 used plastic bottles, which represents six seconds of world consumption. It was part protest and part art installation. It aimed to connect people to a visual representation of the problem: often, unless people see and experience a problem, they don't feel compelled to change their behaviour.

It was really tough collecting all the bottles and getting the labels off them – everyone in the company was tasked with sourcing 500, but that is actually a lot of bottles to find and to schlep to the office and to clean. I ended up scouring recycling plants like Grundon's out near Heathrow and I became absolutely fascinated by what goes on there. It might sound deeply unsexy but recycling plants are actually like wonderful Willy Wonka factories, with suction machines to make the paper fly upwards, magnets to separate out the metal and gaps for the heavier glass to fall to the bottom. Operators sit by the side of the conveyor belts like gamers, picking out the things they can't recycle, like tents and hoses and saucepans, and mixing them up to be burnt in a giant furnace. The whole plant is then powered from the energy that the furnace generates. Companies like Grundon are working at the 'coalface' of recycling and their creativity in finding ways to recycle materials and keep them in circulation is fascinating.

The *I Am A Plastic Bag* project was also not completely unproblematic from an environmental point of view. For example, although I would have loved to keep everything local to Florence, where the bag is made, the fabric had to be made in Taiwan, because at the time that was the only place that had the technology to make it with the recycled coating. And we have trimmed the bag with leather, which was not our starting point but ended up being preferable to the alternatives: recycled leather and vegan leather are both mostly full of plastic. The good news is that there is so much innovation and R&D happening in this field of more sustainable materials: from natural materials like mushroom 'leather' to clever recycled and reclaimed materials like the ones made from abandoned fishing nets. Change is happening fast, and it is exciting to see.

Creativity is not just about pretty pictures; it is solving problems. In fashion terms I am not just interested in the big design statement. I'm interested in the creative energy that specialists are putting into understanding and developing materials: how things stretch and move, how things wear, how things breathe, how we use recycled materials and how we then recycle them. In fashion and in every area of our national life we need creatives to offer more responsible alternatives that work but that also excite people enough to use them. Creativity plus innovation will always play a big part in finding solutions to our most difficult problems, including the environmental challenges we face.

*

I often wonder where ideas come from. To keep my ideas coming, I need to feed my brain. I need to see things, do things. I need to research things, potter about on the internet, follow up something interesting in *National Geographic*, go to exhibitions and museums and so on. I need to not think too hard and let my brain go, to let it run free. Things lodge in my subconscious and then spit themselves out later. But I don't rely on that subconscious process. I would hate to rely on my mess of a brain or even my mess of a camera roll to capture my ideas and offer them up when I need them. Instead I try to log ideas systematically, on a Pinterest board for a particular project or in an album dedicated to germs of ideas that don't fit anywhere in particular. It might be a railing on the Paris metro or the products lined up by the till at a motorway service station. It might be a drawing or a sample someone at the office has worked up. It might be the way someone has written the date on a letter in beautiful calligraphy, or the way a shiny sweet wrapper crinkles. Sometimes it might just be a shape or a colour or a pattern that appeals to me. If it seems like it might relate to whatever the team is working on, I can put it on a shared album too, just ping it to the team and say, 'I love this, I'm not sure why.' Often one of their brains will pick up the idea and play with it. Sometimes I won't do anything with an idea for years and then I'll be going through my ideas bank and I'll think, *Oh, that's quite interesting, I know what I want to do with that.*

I need to feed my brain, and then I need to relax it. Sitting down with nothing in front of me but a delivery date and a blank sheet of paper can feel overwhelming and be counterproductive. It makes me feel like my brain has been bleached and that I will never have another idea ever again. I am much better served if I start with an image of something that interests me and stick it on the wall in front of me to look at. Sometimes it is the combination of the image in front of me and 'not thinking' about it that produces the inspiration. The subliminal exploration of that image while I am, for example, on the phone can be just as useful. And I often find that I form my best ideas when my brain is in what I can only describe as free-fall. I have to be really relaxed, even half-asleep. Then my brain lets go, it is less inhibited; the ideas flow a bit like dreaming.

The idea for our first public project, *Chubby Hearts Over London*, which was a kind of love letter to the city, came to me that way. I knew that I wanted to move away from our twice-yearly Fashion Week catwalk shows. I had started doing shows in 2012 as something new and scary and exciting, and I had loved the creative platform they gave us. Models flew, stages moved. We had created some memorable moments and grabbed people's attention. Now, though, things had moved on. The shows were traditionally for our wholesale buyers (department and speciality stores) and the press. They would come and watch the shows and place their orders, and then there'd be a lag of a few months while the magazines went to press and the bags got made and into the stores. But the internet was starting to disrupt this process. Our traditional audiences of buyers and trade press were being made less relevant, in terms of both distribution and communication, and our consumers were getting frustrated, seeing images of our shows on Instagram and other platforms but unable to buy the products. We wanted to move away from shows that were just for industry insiders and instead find something more inclusive and interactive that could engage more directly with our customers.

I also knew I wanted something to amplify our new 'chubby' collection of quilted, squishy, pillow-like bags, and that whatever we did would happen during Fashion Week, which meant around Valentine's Day. Also, logged somewhere in my ideas bank was a fish-shaped helium balloon that had a little motor that you could operate by remote control. I think I had first seen it on an advert and I had become a bit obsessed with the idea that you might be sitting at the kitchen table minding your own business and in would float a little shark to 'swim' around the room.

The idea came to me as I was drinking a glass of wine and listening to a concert on the South Bank. My mind was in a kind of relaxed free-fall; I wasn't planning what I was going to do tomorrow, or thinking consciously about anything at all. But there had been a terrible terrorist attack in Borough Market a few months earlier and as I looked out at the packed audience, I thought, *London is so resilient*, and then, *Wouldn't it be lovely to create some kind of guerrilla surprise for the city on Valentine's Day*, to salute its strength and spirit.

It went through many iterations but what we ended up with was twenty-nine huge heart-shaped 'chubby heart' balloons suspended from – or squashed within – iconic buildings across London, including Battersea Power Station, Piccadilly Circus, Trafalgar Square and Covent Garden. Probably my favourite was squashed within Wellington Arch. It was very complicated from a logistics point of view and pretty stressful to pull off, but it still makes me smile when I think about it. Like childbirth, you tend to forget the pain after the event.

The ideas I pursue never come from my brain alone. I work very closely with a small, tight team of creatives including Lisa, Matt and Bevan, who I have already mentioned, plus Kate, who is a marketing genius. Kate and I have been 'joined at the hip' (poor Kate) for seventeen years. We often joke that we should write a book called *Airports We Have Known and Loved*, given the number of work trips we've been on together – or 'holidays', as we jokingly call them, because actually they are really fun. This group has always been such a well-oiled collaboration machine that by the end of every project no one can remember who had which idea. So, for example, the autumn after *Chubby Hearts* we created the *Chubby Cloud* installation, which ended up being a four-day installation and programme of events based on clouds, sleep and switching off. We started with the idea of a giant, enveloping, calming beanbag, which was an idea we'd had logged for a while: we had seen a picture somewhere of a white bag – actually air-filled, I think, rather than filled with beans – that looked like a cross between a bouncy castle and a cloud. Then we brainstormed the kinds of events we might be able to build around that. One of us had the idea of putting the beanbag in Banqueting House on Whitehall, so that once people had sunk into it they would be staring up at the exquisite Rubens ceiling and its chubby angels. Someone else suggested a lecture about sleep rhythms. Someone said we should do something about the digital cloud, and what it actually is. Someone – almost certainly me – suggested we should get the Eric Whitacre Singers to perform *Lux Aurumque* and the London Gay Men's Chorus to sing some lullabies. Then it was a question of approaching people, and convincing them to do it. One of them had a book to promote but mostly we just had to persuade them that they would have fun and be involved in something interesting. We ended up with a brilliant programme including meditations, lectures on sleep and art, orchestras, choirs, Claudia Winkleman and Poppy Delevingne reading bedtime stories, and even Zeb Soanes doing a live reading of the shipping forecast.

Sometimes, though, it can be hard to pump out a steady stream of new ideas to order. I was talking once to John Hegarty, the advertising genius and a truly lovely man, and asking him about this – in a roundabout way. I asked: 'Doesn't it drive you crazy when you come up with a brilliant idea for an advertising campaign and you take it to the client and you know because you are an advertising god [because he is] that it's a brilliant idea, perhaps a bit left-field but a gem, but the client says, "No, I don't get it." And then you have to go back to the office and have another great idea?'

John said that this used to be a real problem for him. Until he was having a tennis lesson one day where he was learning to do a lob shot. 'I was practising and practising it and I couldn't do it. Then finally I hit one perfect lob shot. And my coach said, "Right, now we're going to move on to the backhand spin."' John told me he protested. 'But I've only done one good lob shot,' he said. 'Maybe I should keep practising.' But the coach said, 'No. If you've done one good shot, you can do it again.'

John said his tennis lesson helped him understand that, if you can do it once, you can do it again, and this advice has certainly helped me. I think of it often when I'm frightened I have hit a creative block. The point being that if you have a brain that usually spits out ideas, your brain will do it again. That's how your brain works. You just have to trust yourself, not self-sabotage, and believe that you will get there. Lean into the problem, chip away at it bit by bit. And don't panic.

John Hegarty also says that when people want to zig, you should zag. Being creative means not doing what everyone else is doing. It means thinking: *OK, that's how everyone's always done it. How can we do it a bit differently?* It's important to be brave and not do the comfortable thing. That's when you will hit on something.

But in my experience it is not that easy knowing when you have hit on something. Or knowing whether what you have hit on is gold, or solid rock. And whether you should keep on going or stop digging.

In my business, once we decide to pursue a particular idea, we go into it deeply. Let's say it's an idea for a new collection. We do lots of research and play with lots of ideas. We create a physical space full of inspiration from that research and those ideas, so that people can walk in and see the physical embodiment of what we are talking about. Next we draw, draw, draw. Eventually, when we are happy with the drawings, we start to make up the physical objects in salpa – a kind of toile material that moves like leather – so that we are working in 3D. We experiment with sticking things onto the salpa with sellotape, glue, staples, even stitching. Only when we are comfortable with the salpa do we go to our craftspeople with our first prototype and it is then a two-way backwards and forwards, *how about we try* process to get it how we want it before we're ready to cut into the material we are actually planning on using, and finally ordering our showroom samples. Once we've seen the first sample in the right material, we have hundreds of further decisions, big and small. How can we avoid waste and build circularity into the design? What would a responsible supply chain look like? How can we make the product to a price that will ensure its success? Can we keep the bag unlined to keep it lightweight? How do we think the handle attachment should work? What metal hardware should we design? What colour and size of stitching should we use? Do we want green with a red trim? Grey with cobalt blue or cobalt blue with grey? Once all of that is decided, and documented, and all the samples are made up, we can go to market and meet all our customers. We present to them, they make their orders, and we move into production and delivery.

Those are the practical steps in the journey from idea to product. More generally, pretty much every successful idea I have ever had – for a bag, or a show, or a shop design, or a fundraising project – goes through its own creative journey. Once an idea has bubbled up and I've decided to pursue it, it usually goes something like this: *I love it, I love it, I love it – It's great, it's amazing, it's so cool – I'm nervous – I'm bored of it – It's hard – I'm not sure – It's really hard – I hate it – Maybe it's OK – Actually, I really hate it – I hate myself – Maybe if I just – No – Maybe then if I – Actually, it's OK – I like it – In fact, it's great – I love it.*

I start off passionate about an idea, then, about 25 per cent of the way into making it a reality, I usually fall out of love with it. I lose the excitement, because I've got used to the idea. And I hit a rough patch because inevitably the material doesn't work, or I can't achieve the technique I had in mind, or there's some other problem I hadn't anticipated. At this point I can abandon the idea and pick another, or I can stick with the problem. It's really, really hard to know which is the right approach. Of course, not every idea is a good one and not all problems can be overcome. But since all ideas go through this stage – not one single idea gets a completely smooth ride – if you ever want to come out the other side, you have to, most of the time, hold your nerve and stick with the problem.

For example, when I first started thinking about *Chubby Hearts*, my idea, inspired by the helium-filled sharks, was to 'swim' helium-filled hearts around the city. I saw, in my mind's eye, chubby hearts bobbing down the Mall or along the Embankment, making people smile wherever they went. It was immediately obvious that there would be impossible health-and-safety problems with moving massive double-decker-sized balloons around London, but it was a starting point and got us thinking about inflatables. Our next idea was to tie a huge helium-filled heart-shaped balloon to every bridge in London on Valentine's Day as a one-off surprise for the city. I could imagine how beautiful that would look, with red heart-shaped balloons strung out along the Thames. I could imagine people taking pictures from planes as they flew down the river towards Heathrow. The problem was that every bridge is half-owned by one council and half-owned by another. Plus, balloons sway about a lot, and their strings would get tangled up in the bridge infrastructure. It became clear that this too was completely impractical. So we abandoned that idea as well. But we stuck with the problem. We hit on a different approach: more *Where's Wally?*, with balloons springing up, a few each day, in well-loved and recognisable spots all over the city.

We created a visual to help us communicate the project: a bird's-eye view of London, showing a sea of illustrated red heart-shaped balloons popping up over beautiful landmarks, and a bird flying over the top of them, inspired, perhaps, by the idea of people seeing them from the planes above the city.

Then we started to approach iconic buildings, kicking off with Battersea Power Station, partly because Pink Floyd's inflatable pig had famously flown there forty years earlier. To our great delight they said, 'Great, let's do it.'

It got more complicated from there. We realised that landlords only own the land, not the air space above it. So as well as permissions from landlords and councils (who all have their own different processes) and health and safety and in some cases English Heritage, we would also have to get permission from the Civil Aviation Authority (CAA). The CAA needed precise coordinates for every possible location, and ideally three months' notice. But we were already in December, for a February launch, and we didn't yet know which locations would grant us permission, or where precisely in each location would be the best place to fly. We hadn't yet scoped out which corner of Trafalgar Square would work best with the wind, the trees, the sight lines and so on, even if we did get permission to fly there, and it was getting very close to the Christmas break. So we had to bombard the CAA with hundreds of pieces of paperwork to cover all possibilities, which was time-consuming for us and probably very irritating for them (although they were actually very supportive of the project when we managed to find the right person to explain what we were up to).

The whole project required a huge amount of charm, and a big sell. We had to convince all of these people that what appeared to be a bureaucratic headache was actually a fantastic idea for cheering up the city that would make them feel proud. Our bird's-eye illustrated document was extremely helpful in communicating our vision and enthusing the many, many people we needed to get on board. We also worked especially closely with Westminster Council, who were hosting the lion's share of the chubby hearts, and with Justine Simons (London's Deputy Mayor for Culture and the Creative Industries), who was brilliant and helped us to navigate our way through a lot of it.

We had to take account of wind conditions, so every location needed a visit to ensure we weren't in a wind tunnel, and we became obsessed with an app hilariously called PredictWind. Then we realised we had a challenge with anchoring the balloons. It took a long time to work out the best, least logistically complicated, most cost-efficient method of weighing the balloons down, a problem made more complex because we wouldn't know where they needed to be anchored until the day as it would depend on the prevailing wind conditions. In the end my son Hugo had the brilliant idea of using Smart cars, with project-branded hoarding around them. That way we could easily drive the 'anchor weight' to where it was needed with no heavy lifting required. Then we needed parking permits. We were working with twenty-nine locations in seventeen London boroughs and every borough had a different process for parking permits. We had a whole protocol for what would happen if the wind caught a balloon in the wrong way and it started doing a 'nodding donkey', which meant it could bounce around, hitting the ground or, worse, a passer-by. We had a protocol for what would happen if one broke loose. Some of these balloons were the size of double-decker buses and each one had its own operating team. But it all went off smoothly (more or less), over five days, and it was, honestly, magical.

It started as a lovely idea, morphed several times, and ended up entailing a lot of mind-bending logistics. But fundamentally we stayed true to the vision and the original intention. It was the kind of joining-the-dots, problem-solving, making-things-happen creativity that I love.

Going through the creative cycle, from *I love it* via *I hate it* back to *I love it*, never stops being really tough. But it is another example, like doing scary things, where you build up your muscles. It does get easier. I have been through the cycle so many times now that even when I am at the bottom, and hating the idea and hating myself, and wondering whether this is one of the times I really should abort, there is a part of me that knows this is just how the process works and that probably I will get through it.

That doesn't stop me reaching for the wine gums at times and feeling horrid and perhaps even doing dominoes occasionally. But it helps.

Creativity is not just having the original idea. Most of true creativity is getting through the creative cycle, solving the problems and seeing it through. I suspect anyone who has invented something great or designed something beautiful or painted something amazing would agree.

(Incidentally, there is a kind of frivolous-but-also-true alternative creative cycle that goes like this: *I know I've got to do it – I'm not doing it yet but I'm going to start soon – I will start it, I promise – I will start – then, <u>all the work done on the last day while crying</u>*. Sadly that is also quite true of most creatives, in my experience. And it is certainly true right now on a Sunday afternoon as I write this chapter and have to hand it in to my editor tomorrow morning. Why didn't I start earlier?)

The final piece of the creative puzzle for me is creative visualisation. Creative visualisation is a powerful tool that I use both for calming my nerves before standing up to speak and for taking my ideas through the creative cycle from vision to finished product. You don't have to actually do a drawing like I did for my shop. You can create the picture in your head. You could even probably, if you are not a visual person, just write it down and put it somewhere you are going to keep seeing it. It is about setting intentions, being very clear about what you want to achieve and keeping the idea front-of-mind. It is about priorities, and maintaining focus. It keeps you objective, so that by the time you've dealt with all the 'not possible's and solved all the logistical problems, you can check back that you haven't dumbed it down too much, or messed it around too much and lost what was good about the idea in the first place.

The more specific and detailed and vivid your visualisation can be, the better. For example, we recently launched a handbag collection based on rope. I became really interested in the traditional rope-making industries that have been so crucial in our seagoing national story. I loved the fact that these ropes had saved sailors' lives – so technical nous in knot-making had been of life-and-death importance – but had also been a source of creativity and artistry on long boring passages at sea. At the start of the project, I tried to imagine how everything would look at the end. I saw a lovely showroom in Paris full of beautiful bags, with someone sitting in the corner of the room making knots and demonstrating how to do it. I imagined beautiful little trinkets made from rope – a seahorse, a pair of cherries. I imagined different types of sisal. I created a detailed picture in my head and took a snapshot so that I could keep going back to it as the project developed. Then the process involves toggling between the vision and the granular execution, until the big picture joins up with the small and reality matches the idea.

Going back to the vision keeps me focused and helps me not to give up when I've hit one too many brick walls. It is also crucial for communicating the idea to everyone else who you need to engage and enthuse. That is when documenting your vision rather than just keeping it in your head becomes important. It doesn't come naturally to me because I am someone who would always prefer to just crack on, but unless you have a way to share your vision you don't get people on board.

Years ago, I saw a beautiful corner site on Sloane Street and I got it into my head that this would be a perfect place for a store. I really, really wanted it. We did the sums and worked out that this would be a big step for the company but one we were excited to take. The next challenge was: could we persuade the landlord to give us the site? I wanted to find a way to stand out, and also – although I didn't think of it this way at the time – to share with him my creative vision of how wonderful it would be. It was Christmas time and, in a slightly do-or-die frame of mind, rather than just sending him a formal offer letter I sent the letter but also enclosed with it a bespoke advent calendar. It was a drawing of the store (with my name on it) full of handbags, and each little window in the advent calendar opened to show a photo of me holding up a sign saying 'Anya for Sloane Street'. I am pretty embarrassed to share this story but I think at the time I wanted him to know how much I wanted it, and also to convey how beautiful I could make it, and I thought it wouldn't do any harm to make him smile. In a funny way it was an echo of that first drawing I did, aged sixteen. I got the shop.

It doesn't need to be a creative project. If you're in financial services, the vision could be for a new financial product. You could visualise being at an awards ceremony and winning an award for innovation, with a sales team who are proud to wear badges with the new product logo on them, and an advertising campaign that not only drives awareness but also makes everyone feel good about the product.

The point is, you create the vision and then, as you execute and meet all sorts of obstacles and get stuck in all sorts of details, you keep checking back in with the vision, to keep you ambitious and make sure you don't get knocked off track.

I love creating. It's a thrill for me. Having the vision and taking it from start to finish is where I get my kicks. Apart from anything else, creativity feeds my soul. I'd be a bit bored without it.

7

I Would Label My Children If I Could

I have a nerdy fascination with the subject of organisation, from email inboxes right down to sock drawers. A place for everything, and everything in its place.

Being organised is critical to running a business and critical to running a family, and becomes essential when you manage both. I also believe it to be vital to my mental well-being. It is a coping mechanism: a way of finding some sense of control when things feel very much out of control – which, especially in the busy patches of life with a young family, can feel like quite a lot of the time. It is a way of sorting out my thinking: perhaps because of my slight dyslexia, I find visual systems of organisation – colour codes, highlighters, tabs, sections, labels – very helpful. I get a kick out of it too.

My brother bought me a labelling machine as a jokey Christmas present one year. It's a more modern version of the old Dymo ones we had as kids, when we used to label our bedroom doors with 'KEEP OUT!!!' and 'GO AWAY!!!'. The new one is still made by Dymo but now runs on batteries and prints out neat little white sticky labels with black type. I could not love it more and would happily label everything in my house if I had my way – including my children. Pretty much every project I undertake starts with a list and this labelling machine. I think it is hard to be creative without being organised, or at least hard to deliver a successful creative project without organisation.

Projects are one thing, but sometimes even just the day-to-day organisation can be a challenge: managing the relentless digital bombardment of images, messages, information and tasks that we have become used to receiving on so many devices. When I was young and starting out in business, tasks and information could only arrive through the physical post, on the phone or in person. If something was very urgent it might arrive by fax. The post, the phone, people and even faxes tended to keep office hours. Now it's wall-to-wall 24/7 messages via email, text, WhatsApp, Instagram, Slack, Teams, and on and on.

How to deal with digital overwhelm as efficiently and effectively and healthily as possible is something no one in my generation was taught at school. Capturing all of these tasks coming in from so many different sources in real time and turning them into a workable action plan requires skilled dexterity. My children's generation is getting help with this, though. In my oldest son's first week as a trainee lawyer, he was given training in best-practice methods of managing his inbox. I was so curious about it that I contacted the training company and explored what they taught, which was fascinating. I felt that our customers might also be interested, and we ended up running four days of talks and workshops on the subject of organisation in the basement of our Sloane Street store.

We learnt a technique, devised by David Allen and delivered by a company called Next Action Associates, called 'Getting Things Done'. The first central idea is that you make yourself as efficient and time-effective as possible if you take all the incoming – texts, WhatsApps, emails, Slack, things you get tasked with in a meeting, stuff your child shouts down the stairs at you, the school handout at the gate – and immediately put them on one comprehensive to-do list.

But there are lists, and then there are lists. Next Action Associates advise you to organise your new comprehensive to-do list according to where you are going to do each task – at its simplest, this would mean one group of tasks to do at home and another group of tasks to do at work. But they encourage you to go even further and make lists for things you need to do at your computer, lists of phones calls and so on. The idea is that you don't waste time staring at a task you can only do at home while you are at work; similarly, if you are walking from one meeting to another and only have ten minutes, you can scan your phone-call list and knock some of those calls off quickly.

I am a big buyer of all this. Lists help me to feel sane and in control. I believe David Allen's motto that your brain is for 'having ideas, not holding them'. If you can do a 'mind-sweep' and get everything you need to remember out of your brain and onto a list, you can relax in the knowledge that it is all captured and won't be forgotten. There's a kind of relief to it, even though you haven't actually done any of it. Your brain is freed up from spending all its energy trying to remember all the things you mustn't forget – a task it is not very good at, by the way, as we all know from the number of times we arrive home having forgotten to do the one thing we were meant to do, despite having reminded ourselves about it all day. Your calmer, freer, less distracted brain then has the space and energy to think of new ideas or new tasks.

Apparently error 101 is to send yourself an email with a task on it, for instance 'Write thank-you note for Jane'. I am so guilty of this. This task, they say, should go straight onto your to-do list, saving you the unnecessary action of then having to move it to your to-do list later on.

If you are not careful, your email inbox can sometimes look like your to-do list, but treating it like one is a mistake. Not everything in my inbox needs doing, and not everything I need to do is in my inbox. Making my inbox my to-do list risks letting whoever is most trigger-happy at the keyboard set my priorities. So I have to have a comprehensive to-do list somewhere that is separate from my email inbox.

A second key strategy we were taught – which I am still learning – is that if there is something on your list that you keep coming back to again and again but which you never actually get done, you should try thinking about what the next action is. So if you have a broken lamp and no clue what the problem is, it is highly likely you will put 'Fix lamp' on your to-do list. It is also likely that you will look at 'Fix lamp' on your to-do list twenty times and walk past the broken lamp another twenty times before you do anything about it, and each time it is like a slow stab. *Ugh, I still haven't done it.* What you actually need on your list is not 'Fix lamp' but rather 'Buy bulb' or 'Try changing bulb' or 'Speak to electrician' or whatever the actual *next action* is on the path to getting the lamp fixed. Break the task down, be clear what the next action is, and then you are much more likely to take that action and get it off your list and not stay stuck.

And just to ruin your day (sorry), Next Action also insist that your email inbox should always be empty. We should see our email inbox as simply the delivery method, and any tasks that arise should then go onto the comprehensive to-do list. I have completely failed at this,

IF IN DOUBT, WASH YOUR HAIR

although I did like the advice to set up a 'Waiting For' folder in your inbox, so that at least the messages about the Amazon deliveries you are waiting for are not winking at you every time you check your email.

I am a long way from having cracked this system. Clearly, it is a bit of a science and some will adopt it more seriously than others. But some of these tips really helped me and we certainly had full houses for all the tutorials at Sloane Street when we offered them to our customers. I am obviously not alone in needing to find the best way through the digital overwhelm.

This isn't part of the 'system' but in terms of digital overwhelm I've also understood that my conscientious 'ping it straight back' approach to my emails is doing me no favours. A wise friend (yes, the same one who helps me say no to tempting engagements) explained to me: if you are feeling overwhelmed, rather than trying to clear it all – which never works because the more you send, the more you receive – slow down the flow of traffic. Don't immediately answer every email. Don't be the first one to answer every query on the WhatsApp group for your child's class at school. Maybe even just don't answer some messages at all.

I find this advice difficult to follow. When it comes to my emails I'm the person jumping up and down on the balls of my feet, tennis racket at the ready: send me an email, I'll fling you one straight back. Ask thirty parents what we should buy the kids' teacher for Christmas and I immediately reply with a suggestion. Even if the request is an unreasonable one, I'll always try to return it. But the problem then is you get into these endless exhausting rallies. I need to accept that sometimes I have to conserve my energy and let the odd one go, even though it goes against the grain.

In those Sloane Street workshops we also tackled the subject of decluttering. Most of us are lucky enough to have too much stuff. This has got to change for lots of reasons. But not many of us have cracked it yet and so, especially if we have children, who seem to accumulate clutter faster than anyone else, unless we are disciplined enough to cull and edit and shelve and archive, we can end up drowning in it all.

According to Parkinson's law, work expands to fill the time available to complete it – so if you wait until the last minute, it only takes a minute to do. It seems that data also expands to fill the space available for storage, and people accumulate stuff to fill the space they have to house it.

I am not good with clutter. I find puddles of things all over the place suffocating. I find calm in looking at a little bit of empty space on a shelf, and knowing that my cupboards aren't all bursting. I think we all need some empty space in our homes and the capacity to be able to put things away. Or perhaps not: it seems that many of my family members (mentioning no names!) would be very happy having puddles of things around the house and on the kitchen table at all times.

Our workshops were given by Gill Hasson, who wrote the book *Declutter Your Life,* and focused on our emotional connections to things and the emotional reasons – fear, hope, nostalgia and guilt – why things we don't want or need or use still end up occupying precious space in our homes.

Sometimes we find it difficult to let go of something because we worry we might need it in the future. Sometimes an item represents a person we one day hope to be: we hope that one day, when we have more time or energy, or when we lose weight, or when the children leave home, we will read it, wear it, use it. There are things we can't let go of because they represent precious memories, of people we used to know or places we used to go or things we used to do. And then there are the things that we feel guilty about giving away: gifts from our parents/ children/friends, clothes we have barely worn, books we think we ought to read, maybe even family heirlooms that you would never use but you would feel heartless giving away.

There are strategies for dealing with each of these emotions. In reality, if in a month or a year or five years you find you need something you have given away, you can probably borrow another one, or buy one second-hand. In reality, owning things that you would use if you were different will not make you different, it will just remind you of what you are not getting around to doing. Focus on enjoying the things you need for who you are now. Be selective and deliberate (and organised) about the memories you keep. Don't allow gifts or heirlooms to become burdens, and separate your feelings for the people who gave them to you from your feelings about the things themselves.

Perhaps what I find most helpful of all, when I am struggling to part with things, is to be very conscious of where a thing is going next, and to think about how lovely it is to put that thing back into circulation, where someone else can make use of it and take pleasure from it. So that vegetable spiraliser that was a gift from your children and which you have never used perhaps represents a laudable desire to eat more vegetables. But instead it is taking up storage space, and making it harder to get to other things you do use, and keep everything clean and tidy. And you are in fact eating no more wafer-thin courgette than you would if you didn't own it. Yes, it was expensive, and yes, you are grateful to your children for the thoughtful gift, but if you are not using it, give it away so that someone else can use it and take pleasure from it. Let it go.

For me, 'like with like' is another key to reducing the overwhelm of stuff. I don't like not knowing what I own and buying a new something because I've forgotten I already have one. If I keep light bulbs with light bulbs, batteries with batteries (and, fair warning, I may murder the next child who puts the dead batteries back with the undead ones), cables with cables, then there is just one place to look and if we have it I will find it.

The same goes for paperwork. It helps to have an area set aside for paperwork, full of labelled files: one for instruction manuals, one for guarantees, one for each child. The children's boxes started off being full of the paperwork about their health checks, then it was letters from their schools and now they each just have one file that houses their birth certificates, exam certificates, national insurance numbers, NHS numbers and so on, so that there is one place to go to. I even have a box for orders of service, from weddings and funerals. I love keeping those, for sentimental reasons but also for inspiration as and when.

My pet hate are drawers that contain a mix of a light bulb, some batteries, three stamps, a pen lid, a 10p coin, a high-denomination-but-what-is-it-worth note from Uzbekistan and a cable of unknown origin and function. They make me feel a bit queasy, but more importantly they waste time when you are trying to find something.

Being uncluttered and keeping 'like with like' doesn't mean you have to be heartless, or that you can't keep special things you are attached to. So, for example, I have a memory shelf in my wardrobe, where I keep sentimental items of clothing that I will likely never wear again but which I don't want to give away, along with my wedding dress, of course. And memory boxes – both digital and physical – are important to me. My digital memory box is a folder on my computer where I keep emails that make me smile or lift me up in some way. My physical one is full of funny little notes from the children, handmade birthday cards, special invitations and so on. I have one box per year and the contents grow as the year goes on, and then things are easy to locate when I need them or want to sift through them again for the pleasure it brings. The children also each have boxes for their own memories, and their many 'precious' pieces of artwork. When the kids were growing up, we had the 'special cupboard' for them to 'display' their finest (and endless) coil pot collections. It has been the source of much amusement and ribbing over the years as it was actually the bottom shelf in James's bathroom cupboard. 'No greater honour,' we would say.

Something I found that I couldn't bear to get rid of was my children's many pairs of tiny and then not-so-tiny Converse shoes. They have all worn Converse since they were little and I had a collection of about forty pairs, from tiny ones with Velcro fastenings for a baby who clearly couldn't even walk to enormous mud-covered ones that had tramped around Tibet. I could always tell just from looking at them exactly who had worn them: the shoes seemed to take on the character of the child. And I just couldn't quite bring myself to throw them out. I ended up displaying them all in one enormous frame, from smallest to biggest. It makes me smile every time I pass it.

I am guilty of being tidy, and I am prone to a cull. 'She's probably thrown them away' is the constant accusation at home. But deep down I am pretty sentimental and will keep and even give pride of place to things that hold precious memories. I just don't want them in puddles all over the surfaces!

Given the industry I work in, I also try to see wardrobe planning as part of my job. It sometimes feels superficial, and a bit of a slog, but if I treat it this way (as a job) and get this part of my life sorted, it keeps my head clear for more important things. It means I can avoid the early-morning meltdowns, unable to find anything to wear when I have to be out of the door in ten minutes; I can quieten the distracting outfit-choice-related noise in my head, and be reassured that I am going to feel comfortable and appropriate – and therefore confident – whether I'm scrabbling around in the warehouse, hanging out in the office or heading to a meeting full of fashion people where I know I will be judged.

The way it works best for me is if I pull everything out of my wardrobe and put it on a fold-out rail I bought from Amazon. That way I am committed, and I can only put back into the wardrobe clothes I am *actually* wearing at the moment – rather than those that haven't been worn in years. Often what I find as I am doing this is that I have lots of 'almost-outfits' that are missing a component – say, a jumper. Then I have to decide: is this outfit special enough to justify investing in a jumper to go with it? And if not, am I ever going to wear the rest of it? Or perhaps I realise that there's a shirt I love that goes with everything but I never wear it because the sleeves are too long. So, better to get it altered. Get that missing button sewn on, buy that sweater. There is no point having a load of half-outfits clogging up your wardrobe and wasting time in the morning as you try to work out what to wear.

Then I put everything that I'm not wearing at the moment away somewhere else. And what I am left with is a load of outfits that I like wearing and that I don't have to think about again until the next wardrobe session.

Someone in my industry who I worked with once shared a tip she uses, which is to actually lay each outfit out, complete with shoes, belt, handbag, earrings, everything. Then take a photo and put it in an album on your phone called 'Outfits'. I can then lie in bed in the evening and quickly choose what I'm going to wear the next day from this album. In the morning I can jump up, throw on the outfit and get going. And if, for example, I have a trip to Japan with two press days, four dinners, a traipsing day and two travel days, I can flick through the album, check nothing is in the wash or at the dry-cleaner's, and quickly pull together everything I need.

Packing, for me, is like a bigger, more headachy version of getting dressed in the morning. I have to pick not one outfit but several, and there are so many decisions to make, each of which can make a huge difference to my comfort and mood if I get it wrong.

For example, on one typical day recently I was in Hong Kong, traipsing around shopping centres and outside locations for a new project. I needed my hair back so it wouldn't go into a complete frizz. I needed flat shoes for the traipsing and shoes with a heel for a meeting later. I needed an outfit that went with both the flats and the heels; that covered me for freezing air-conditioned interiors and incredible humidity outdoors; and that, without being too try-hard, would demonstrate that I spoke the silent nuanced language of fashion. My husband was with me and he just went with navy trousers and a white shirt. I had four outfit changes and a spreadsheet.

One of our bestselling product lines, our Labelled collection, came out of my hate-hate relationship with packing. There's a bag labelled 'Make-Up', another labelled 'Cables and Chargers', one that's called 'Suncreams' and so on. There's a little pouch marked 'Pounds', one that says 'Dollars' and another that's 'Yen'. Plus one that says 'Receipts', for making claiming expenses less painful. So if I had grabbed all the right bags, and pulled out the cash from the right pouch so I had coins for the trolley at the airport, I could relax knowing I hadn't forgotten anything crucial. I wasn't going to wind up getting out my laptop in a hotel room only to realise I was missing a wire. Of course, you don't need branded bags – you just need a system.

I do feel a bit of a loser being so systematic about it all, but I have accepted that it makes me feel better when I know I have all of this nailed.

It also saves me money because I stop buying things that I don't need, or that don't go with anything else I own. And it makes it very obvious which is the stuff that I never wear any more. Wardrobe clear-outs are a win-win activity. That item that actually slightly pulls in the wrong place or that doesn't work with anything else and is taking up precious space in your wardrobe or drawer can be passed on to someone else who will enjoy wearing it. Give it to a friend, take it to a charity shop, sell it on eBay. Meanwhile, you will be left with a wardrobe full of clothes that you actually want to wear. If you can afford a professional to do this with you, that's amazing. If not, find the kind of friend who can tell you honestly when something isn't doing it for you any more and offer the reciprocal service to them.

I realise that not everyone works in fashion and worries about clothes. But I think a lot of us have something that is taking up too much headspace and that could be fixed with a bit of planning. It might be the weekly family meals. A similar approach – periodically logging meals that everyone likes and healthy snacks that can be eaten in meetings, then plotting them for each week – can work. Maybe it's maintaining the house: the gutters, the boiler, the windows. Make a plan, set reminders, get ahead of it.

It's hard not to make the connection between organising and handbags. Handbags quite simply are for being organised and having what you need when you leave the house. Even as a child I loved little compartments and drawers and zips and pockets, and I have always found something really exciting about getting a new bag and putting all your things in the pockets. Thirty-five years since my mother gave me my first handbag, I still get a deep thrill from organising my things this way. So with every bag that I design, just as much as I pay obsessive attention to making it a beautiful object, I also obsess about making it work: making it a bag where there is a place for everything and you won't have to go scrabbling around to locate it. We are busy people. We are travelling, schlepping, trying to be good parents, trying to be good businesspeople, trying to do all the right things. Being organised in our lives, with our things in the right places, can give us the space to think clearly, make us feel more in control, help us to stretch that precious resource of time a little bit further.

Being organised does, in itself, take time, of course. I have not been able to find a better solution to organising my life yet than working on a Sunday afternoon, which I do regard as a bit of a fail. During the week I can usually deal with anything easy and everything important, but anything slightly more complicated or anything that is a long read gets put aside for Sunday. If I put time aside on a Sunday, it means I can clear my inbox of whatever didn't get dealt with during the week, and I can hand things over to various bits of the business on a Monday morning. If I have seen the bottom of my inbox, I feel ahead of the game: I feel like I have washed my hair.

Once I have cleared the debris of the week just gone, Sunday afternoons are also my time for looking ahead and planning. It is helpful to consider how this week's priorities have moved on during the week. I spend time thinking about whether last week's priorities are still this week's priorities, and I redo my to-do list. It's just a time to pause and take stock.

This is also the time for getting ahead with the life admin. Booking a holiday, buying a birthday present for a godchild, writing the thank-you letters, working out how each child is going to get where they need to be through the week, looking at my own forward diary and making sure I have cut out enough stepping stones and made time for the gym. And if I can find a way of ticking off two things in one time slot – getting a manicure with a friend, or having a walking meeting – that always feels like a huge win.

I do sometimes feel resentful about losing 20 per cent of my weekend to this, but I have not been able to find another way at this busy stage of my life. I would love to be a go-with-the-flow person who didn't need to plan and could have fun all weekend but it just doesn't feel possible at the moment. Someone suggested I could do everything I do on a Sunday on a Friday instead. I did try blocking out my Friday afternoons as 'desk time', but somehow this didn't seem to work. I'm tired by Friday and my head just isn't in the right space. Whereas on a Sunday, after a weekend off, I'm more: *Right, let's crack on!*

It is not easy to do, and when I was in the small-children-bubble phase it was nigh on impossible, but organising myself and planning ahead is also key for me to exercise and eat healthily. I think of it as my present (planning) self outsmarting my future (eating and exercising) self. If I have the right foods in the fridge and I make up my lunch and some healthy snacks before I leave the house, I am much less likely to power through lunchtime without eating, then suddenly realise I am ravenous at 3 p.m. and attack the birthday cake left lying around in the office. I can feel my energy is longer and stronger and more balanced and my mood is better all day, whereas the 3 p.m. cake leaves me feeling furious and horrible. Or if I know I am going for drinks in the evening I can try to eat something healthy before I leave, so that I'm not simply grabbing the canapés being handed round without even noticing I'm eating them. If I have planned a walk with a friend, or booked a gym session and put it in the diary, or even just committed to myself that a particular time slot is when I am going to exercise every day, obviously I am far more likely to actually do it.

The same went for organising my children when they were small. Yes, the constant communication. The shared diary, whether on a blackboard on the kitchen wall or on an iPad displayed somewhere prominent. Sharing childcare with a friend during the school holidays. Beat the clock. Having the class rep from your child's school enter all the term dates and concert dates and fixture dates and whatever else into a shared diary that everyone can download. The Christmas Contract.

But the key to organising life with lots of children, for me, was looking ahead. Yes, it eats into my Sunday, and yes, I have taken a lot of flak on this from the other members of my family, but if I wasn't thinking ahead then life quickly got pretty uncomfortable. I feel relaxed reaching out and asking another mother for help with a lift somewhere in ten days' time. I feel awful leaning on someone to divert and collect my children this afternoon. I feel OK (well, sort of) telling the children in advance that we are going to be on a business trip for their year assembly but that Granny will be there to represent us and will take them out for pizza afterwards. By contrast, I feel awful when I suddenly throw it at them, saying, 'Oh, I'm not going to make the assembly tomorrow and I haven't organised an alternative.' They feel let down and cross and the knock-on effect is more hassle than being organised in the first place.

When I had little children at home and a nanny, we would do the forward look together. I made it a planned weekly meeting, not something done in a rush as I came in the door and she was tired and wanting to go home. That half an hour or hour that we carved out every week saved me from so many crises, mostly small, but all time-consuming and distracting and the kinds of things that could tip me over the edge in a busy week and make me feel really bad.

Being organised takes effort and energy but I actually think a busy life takes effort and energy anyway. It's just a question of timing, and mostly that is within my control. I can choose to get ahead, which does take more effort up front, or I can choose not to and accept that I will spend that same energy scrambling to catch up. It is often even more exhausting not having things sorted than just sorting them out. Of course, there is a point where being over-organised can get very boring and kill the fun (and the fun of those around you). But equally, not being organised and having everything constantly falling apart quickly gets old for everyone involved too. You have to find the piece of middle ground that works for you, but the point is that, mostly, you can choose. For me, it is a conscious decision to place the energy at the start because I feel so much better when I am on top of things. I like feeling prepared and, more importantly, I don't like how it feels when I am unprepared.

8

Be Yourself; Everyone Else is Already Taken

I remember coming across this quote, popularly attributed to Oscar Wilde: 'Be yourself; everyone else is already taken.' It gave me pause for thought because, looking back over the years, I realise it took me too long to know, and accept, and be, who I really am.

I think we all have different versions of ourselves that we get out for different occasions, to respond to different situations. And that's fine – it's normal; even quite clever. But it's only in the last few years that I've found and made peace with my core, most true self. Before then I would try out different versions of myself and most of them felt like equally possible versions of me. Now I feel like I've found my happy place – the place where I am genuinely myself. I'm not uncomfortable, I'm not operating at a level that is unsustainable, I'm not trying to be more entertaining, or tougher, or braver, than I feel I can naturally be.

It's like taking off a pair of high-heeled shoes and an 'effort' of an outfit and putting on a favourite pair of trainers and a comfy coat, but sometimes I wish I had got there sooner. The sooner you can be content about who you are rather than who you wish you were, the more confident and relaxed and the happier you will be. And that is about knowing what really makes you happy and what really doesn't; knowing what you need to keep the stress levels about right for you; understanding your core values; and knowing what you are good at, what you need to accept about yourself, and what you need work on. Also, be your own judge. Learn not to care about what anyone else thinks. Not in an unkind way, but more 'just be yourself', or 'you do you', as my kids would say.

Here are a few things I have discovered about me.

I am not cool and I am a bit serious. I like a sad movie more than a comedy.

I have a big nose but I have grown to quite like it because it is my father's nose and I like my father.

I accept that I am unlikely ever to be the thinnest girl in the room.

I would love to be extroverted and entertaining and sociable, but actually I am a bit shy. My favourite evening is at my kitchen table with close friends and family (but I often need half an hour on my own with a newspaper too). I don't really like drinks parties or tiny talk or red-carpet look-at-me moments.

I have a thing for choral music, and big choirs move me to tears.

I was impatient in the classroom but I am not stupid.

I don't like feeling out of control and I like to be organised (to the point of being a complete bore at times – in fact, I even bore myself on occasion).

I have a creative brain.

I am good at the big picture but do better to delegate the granular detail – unless it is creative detail.

I am prepared to take tough decisions and I am steely and determined and persistent in pursuit of what I feel is the right thing to do, but I care deeply about being kind and being fair.

I like to be successful and the lovely things success can provide but I prefer working from passion than for profit.

I have to talk things through to work out what I'm thinking, like combing out a knot or unpicking a tangle of necklaces.

I get a kick from creating beautiful things and a thrill from making things happen – the bigger and scarier the better.

I often get as much happiness from the wanting and the working towards and the striving as from the having. I have to remind myself to enjoy the process because often, on reflection, that is the best bit.

Family is my foundation but my work family comes a close second.

I am extremely self-disciplined, except when it comes to food.

I have come to all of these conclusions largely through experience. But experience takes time, and wouldn't we all rather start living as our true selves sooner than later?

Here are some of the things I wish I had known sooner.

I have come to the realisation that a lot of the doubt I feel – and I know I am not alone – comes from being surrounded by images of unrealistic ideals as defined by other people. These self-appointed decision-makers and gatekeepers determine what is cool, what is in and what is out, what is acceptable and what is not. They keep us unsatisfied and they make us feel we don't belong. It begs the question of why we are letting people dictate these 'ideals' to us in the first place.

This is especially true when it comes to body confidence. I remember the agent of one of the world's most famous – and extremely skinny – models once reassuring me that the woman in question didn't have an eating disorder and was at her normal weight. She had just been born with fine bones and a fast metabolism, as lots of models are. The agent likened models to 'colts' rather than 'carthorses'. But how do the carthorses feel if the only images they ever see are of the colts? As for images of people with different skin tones, older people, people with differently abled bodies and so on: they are even harder to find.

I am ashamed to say that I'm guilty not only of absorbing these subliminal body-shaming messages but also of perpetuating some of them in the decisions I make in my own work. It is hard for any of us to change perceptions that have been lifelong in their reinforcement. But I am hopeful that we are at a moment now where more and more people are starting to understand, question and unpick these harmful dynamics. More and more people are calling for change in the images they are surrounded with. And at the same time more and more people are taking what control they can and deciding to ignore the images, to stop caring about what someone else tells them they ought to care about and to be themselves. This is a daily struggle for me and pretty much everyone I know, but it is a fight that's worth fighting because the moment you stop caring about the old rules is the moment you start having fun.

While, honestly, I still haven't cracked just 'not caring' about how my body looks in a bikini – I am someone who nearly bailed out of a family trip-of-a-lifetime when I realised I was going to have to spend it wearing a shortie wetsuit that played to all my insecurities about my body – I have finally understood that beauty is not about how good you look, but about how good you feel.

In fact, it has always been the mood-altering, confidence-giving aspects of my industry that have interested me. Not fashion per se, or owning the right brands, but the way fashion makes us feel. When I was sixteen, my mother allowed me to borrow one of her handbags. I actually can't remember what it looked like but I still have a visceral memory of how that beautiful piece of craftsmanship made me *feel*: sophisticated and powerful, somehow. Finding that piece, that thing, that makes you feel like the best version of yourself – makes you stand a bit taller, makes you smile with more of your face – that confidence boost is worth something. It's like an actor slipping on the right pair of shoes and suddenly really feeling the part.

So if you were not born with tiny bones and a fast metabolism, make peace with the fact that you are not going to be super-skinny. Focus instead on what is great about you.

It helps to surround yourself with other people who see this the way you do. If you want to avoid wasting headroom on the wrong stuff, be around other people who feel the same. Stay around people who value what you value and therefore make you feel good about yourself.

Controversially, I think that social media can actually help here too. There is a lot of anxiety about its impact on young people and their mental health, and that danger needs to be taken seriously, and addressed, but I also see it as a fascinating and promising new vehicle. Social media allows us all to bypass the magazines and their impossibly skinny size-zero models – some of them genuinely genetically fine-boned, some of them underweight, but all of them in an extremely tiny subset of extremely tiny people – and to follow whoever we like. And there are some brilliant young people out there saying, 'Look at this: this is the Instagram me and this is the real me.' It's empowering to people who have felt excluded by the uniformity and 'perfection' of magazine imagery. It has allowed new messaging about celebrating real bodies and healthy bodies rather than unhealthily thin bodies, or bodies that are for most people genetically unattainable. The standards aren't being dictated by a few editors of a few magazines – they are self-generated by people of all shapes and sizes and body types and ages and skin colours, snapping away in their bedrooms. And the rhetoric is changing from 'Are you thin? Are you thin? Are you thin?' to 'Are you healthy? Are you strong? Does your body do what you need it to?' I hope this takes us to a better world where your individual body shape becomes the equivalent of having long hair or short hair, blue eyes or brown. A different look, rather than the measure of your beauty and virtue.

There is a lot more work to be done on this but the point is that there is beauty in diversity, and inclusivity is imperative if we want to be happy and fair. I have been laughing to myself recently on the endless Zoom calls I'm on at the moment. Online meetings are completely democratising. The girl with the skinny legs no longer holds sway as her ankles are not even in the frame. Ha!

Another thing I wish I had known sooner was to beware of thinking you want something just because everyone else seems to be scrambling after it. I have found that the things I think might be glamorous often really aren't. And the things I think might satisfy me often really don't.

Of course, we all need to provide some basics for ourselves. At the most fundamental level, that is food and shelter. But be careful about assuming that, beyond a fairly modest level, striving for more things – a flashier car, more decadent parties to attend – is going to make you happier. I know a lot of very privileged people who have all that stuff and are very unhappy. Because if accumulating things and being glamorous is your aim, you are never going to win. You will never have enough. There will always be someone wealthier. There will always be a more over-the-top party. There is nowhere to stop.

I have been lucky enough in my life to do some really extraordinary things: trips, events, Fashion Week parties full of designers and supermodels and famous people. The invitations are so beautiful and so tempting, but often those experiences are not what make me happy. If I am honest with myself, I'm a lot happier with a cosy dinner at home with my real friends or a walk in the park.

And I suspect a lot of the other people there are not being made happy by these parties either. They are there because they think they should be happy being there. They are looking round the room at everyone else and worrying that they are not beautiful enough, or thin enough, or interesting enough, or wealthy enough, or successful enough. And not only do they not feel happy there, they then feel guilty about not being happy, because it is supposed to be a privilege to be there. For people who have never been to those parties and perhaps never will, it's important to know that many of them (though not all of them) are deeply unfun.

It was quite a nice moment for me when this realisation dawned and I could say, 'I am going to make the best of these amazing experiences but it is OK if I find them more like work than fun.' I came to realise I am actually much happier with simpler things. I wanted to strive for more nights at my kitchen table. When I sit down with my team or with my family or with friends and we are laughing late into the night over takeout roast chicken and a bottle of red wine, that's gold dust for me. I wanted to work towards more walks-in-the-park-then-coffee with my girlfriends; more ridiculous, pointless-trying-to-explain, all-my-children-leaning-into-each-other in-jokes on the family WhatsApp group. There was one lovely example where I was sitting in an important meeting and one of my younger kids messaged on the family WhatsApp to say he was lost in London and couldn't work out which tube to take. I couldn't reply, but watching the barrage of wittily abusive help he received from his siblings, sending him in the right direction while gently deriding his sense of direction, gave me more pleasure than I can say. Truly, ask me what I want for Christmas and it's that.

To speed up the process, you can approach this like a project. Take a piece of paper and write down all the times and places you remember feeling really good. What was the event, who were you with, what were you doing? Write down where and when you feel most comfortable. Where did you last have a really good laugh? Where did you last feel really relaxed? Where were you last when you felt completely unselfconscious? Then try to join the dots. What have these times got in common?

If you have never done one, it can also be a revelation to do one of the many 'personality tests' that are out there. At work we all did Myers–Briggs (which actually looks at preferences rather than some kind of set or 'true' personality). Someone in my team suggested it, to his great credit. I adored him, and we had worked together for years, but we were struggling to find level footing on work projects. When we had done the test and looked at our results, we started to understand why. He and I were in completely opposite corners of the grid. He was an extreme in the top left-hand box, and I was an extreme in the bottom right-hand box. (Or vice versa. I can't remember now, because I am a big-picture person. He was the details guy.) It became immediately clear what the problem was: I was all about having an idea and getting going with it, finding a way round the problems as we encountered them. He was all about stopping and planning and anticipating all the possible problems before we got there. Just knowing this helped us to understand each other. We realised we were each fulfilling important functions and actually really needed each other to make things work.

Myers–Briggs helped us to understand and accept both ourselves and each other. It helped me to understand why I react in certain ways to certain situations, and that other people just don't, and how that is a good thing. It also helped me understand my impact on other people. My persistence and determination (and organisation!) can be experienced by others as annoying and exhausting. Oh dear.

Another of these tests, based on Myers–Briggs, is 16Personalities, which is really fun and worth doing at home with your family. Try it. It's entertaining but also helpful to understand the character traits you all have and to see how the different personalities work best together.

Having said that, many families unconsciously assign roles to family members that are uninvited and restrictive, yet difficult to shake off. As a child, were you deemed to be the responsible one? The unreliable one? The funny one? The clever one? Do you find yourself falling back into that version of yourself – perhaps a version that no longer feels like the real you – when you are back with your family? Many people find on examination that they do not match the role and characteristics they were assigned as a child.

It's important to realise that we also change as we age. Your personality might be relatively fixed but the things that make you happy might be different at different stages of your life. When you are young, perhaps it's your friends, then the right job, then a partner, then a mortgage, then enough success at work to pay the mortgage. I do enjoy striving, but I have to keep checking back to make sure I'm not striving for something that was right for then but doesn't matter to me any more.

The lockdown and the other changes to all of our lives that came with the pandemic in 2020 were dreadful in so many ways. Loved ones were lost, educations disrupted and businesses and livelihoods destroyed. But for some people – me included – it was also a chance to get off the seemingly out-of-control merry-go-round: to sit still for a bit, and take stock. It brought many of us face-to-face in a quite forceful way with what really matters.

For me, my first priority was my family. I wanted to gather all my children home to me, and to 'lock up' my parents and make sure they were getting everything delivered and had no reason whatsoever to leave the safety of their house. And second was my other family, the people who work in my business. I wanted to make sure they were all OK: to make sure they were healthy, and to do everything I could to protect their jobs so that they were financially healthy too. After that I looked at what I could do to help more widely. I signed up to be an NHS Volunteer and found some ways that our business could help. I swore that after Covid I would not let the planet slip down my agenda.

There were the things I missed terribly: hugging my parents, sitting across the table from my friends, the buzz of the office.

And then there were the silver linings. I can't be the only person to have taken secret delight in deleting things from my diary and spending precious time with my children during their enforced lockdown with us. Three of my children came home and, locked up with no distractions, it was the first time in years, if ever, that we had spent such a concentrated period together. At the same time, the nightly seven o'clock FaceTime calls with my two 'missing' children, my brother and sister and my locked-down parents, was a lovely new ritual. The consolation prize I was being offered was the opportunity for my family to regroup. We may never have that time again.

My friendships deepened too. When we couldn't see each other we exchanged endless WhatsApp messages – from the struggle to lock down our wayward parents to how to cover our greys – and it brought us closer. We were all going through a lot of the same things. I realised too that the friends I kept up with during that time were all that I could really manage in any meaningful sense.

In its own, horrible way, Covid-19 has been good for the planet. It has grounded planes, stopped trains and cars, shut down fossil fuel factories and made everyone consider the length and vulnerability and unsustainability of their supply chains. There is an opportunity to use this rupture in our normality as a bit of a new start. How can we, as we go back to 'normal' life, maintain some of the changes that made things better? We're clearly not going to say we'll never get on a plane again but there are small changes we can all make that collectively would create a big difference. That said, poverty and economic recession threaten to put the needs of the planet further down everyone's to-do list. It is going to be an almighty challenge. Would we – will we – make the same personal sacrifices for the health of the incredible earth we live on as we have for Covid, which is a much less significant threat to human life, albeit a more immediate one?

Living through this extraordinary time has made me reassess my values and whether I am living up to them. Of course it would be easiest to go back to where I was. That's the muscle I am used to exercising. But if we come out of this as we went in, we have missed the point. Never waste a good crisis, they say. There is nothing good about Covid, but we mustn't waste the important opportunities it has given us to reset. So actually, I am going to try very hard to resist the temptation to go back to where I was, and I am writing down – and I urge you to do the same – the insights the situation has given me and the things that, secretly, guiltily, I have enjoyed about it and that I think I should continue with.

As the lockdown lifts, I want to properly embrace working from home and flexible working for me and my company. I have been thinking about it for years but I was always nervous. And the fact is, we have proved that it can be done. I think as we return to 'normal', that normal will include much more of this. We will all find it more ridiculous than ever before that everyone is supposed to travel to work on public transport all at the same time, to sit in expensive urban office space in the middle of London. And we will all have learnt a lot about what rhythms of working are best for us. I have understood that, left to myself, the right rhythm for my day is to get up, exercise, breakfast and then hit the office at ten o'clock and work through until seven. Exercising in the morning is a game changer for me. It is going to be difficult because I know I will feel guilty and lazy if I only make it into the office at ten, but I hope I can quieten that voice in my head and stick to the rhythm that works best for me.

We have always bought some of our food locally but over the last few months we have found ways to really embrace this. We won't go back.

I want to keep digital at the top of my to-do list even as my stores reopen, because that's the future.

I know it's going to be easy for me to go back to filling my diary with appointments but I now realise that my life had become a bit unsustainable. I was 'on' all the time. I'm not off now, I'm still working incredibly hard, but I see now that some of what I was doing before was unnecessary. Having experienced how much I get done in a day when I'm not always running from meeting to meeting, and how much happier I am having more space in my days to focus, and more time at home with my family, I will find it easier than I used to to say no. Why did I fill my diary with so many meetings and travel when there are many clever ways to communicate without the drain to personal well-being, pocket and planet?

Actually, I feel more balanced in myself now than I can ever remember feeling. If you could take away the horrible and scary side of this, there have been many benefits for me. I have learnt a lot about myself and what I did and didn't miss. I need to think about how I carry some of that over when life returns to its new normal.

Once you work out who you really are, and what is going to make you happy, you can lean into that.

And if you surround yourself with people who make you feel like your best self, you can work out the person you become when you are with this individual, or that group of people. Consider which is the true, core, best you. I know there are people who make me feel like a child or an outsider or just not quite comfortably myself. When I'm with them I will be endlessly aware of my hands, and my posture, and what expressions are on my face. And then there are the people who laugh at your jokes and leave you feeling more alive. You're not thinking about whether your elbows are on the table or whether your hands are on your chin. Consciously seek those people out. Spend more time with them.

If parties are your thing, accept every invitation you can. And if one-to-one conversations are your thing, turn down the parties and make time for more of those. If you thrive on socialising, build as much of that as possible into your life. If you need downtime and off-time to replenish your batteries, be ruthless about planning that in.

Take my love of choral music. I have loved classical choral music since I was a child. Before my trauma with the singing competition, I wanted to sing professionally. But it is only recently that I have fully, publicly embraced this part of my personality for fear of being uncool. And since then it has given me so much pleasure. If only I had stopped caring about what people think a bit earlier.

I especially love male voice choirs. I used to ask, every time we organised a show, 'How about a male voice choir?' And every time I would be told no. No, Anya, no. And then one time we did a show about the graphics of the motorway and I asked rather tentatively, 'Is it time now? For a male voice choir?' And it was. We had the 'Pilgrims' Chorus' rearranged by Stephen Brooker, and a 100-voice male choir came on in high-vis vests and it was spine-tingling.

Now James and I, with a couple of wonderful and equally nerdy friends, have started heading out on wintry evenings to beautiful ancient candlelit churches, to listen to choirs like the Tallis Scholars or The Sixteen sing things like Gregorio Allegri's *Miserere* or Thomas Tallis's *Spem in alium* (in forty parts) or *The Lamb* by John Tavener or anything by John Rutter or *Lux Aurumque* by Eric Whitacre. We always go to the pub for wine and pork scratchings beforehand and then we sit there in a really happy winey state of mind and we can be home and tucked into bed by 9 p.m. Bliss.

Or take my creative projects at work. I have realised that I love doing big, slightly stressful, exciting, challenging projects. I get a kick from them because I love pushing myself. I love the feeling when I'm doing a big project and it's all about to launch, and all the communications are set up, and all the installations and all the product is ready to go. I always have a moment of standing in the shower on the day of launch of any big project and feeling the blood rush around my body. It's terrifying but I have also learnt that it's exhilarating.

And I truly believe that, while a little dose of 'fake it to make it' never goes amiss, authenticity is what we need to be aiming for in our personal and business lives. Authenticity is what really resonates with people and allows you to make a true connection. The more passionate I feel about a project, the more authentic I can be about it, and the more successful it tends to be. When I am genuinely passionate about something I am more likely to communicate really openly and honestly and also to enthuse other people. If I am authentic and enthusiastic, people tend to get excited with me. I can get momentum. So I no longer start off projects aspiring to success. I start off thinking: *What do I really care about? What do I really want to do?* Success is a lovely by-product.

It was the same with the decision to buy back my business.

In 2011, I took the big step of leaving the role of Chairman, CEO and Creative Director of my company to become just its Chairman and Creative Director, bringing in a CEO to run the business. I didn't have the time to do all these jobs well and though I found it hard to work out whether I wanted to be CEO and bring in a Creative Director or vice versa, in the end I decided I would focus on the creative side of the business as that role was less easy to hire externally. It felt grown-up and, after twenty years, like an exciting step in the journey of the business. It gave me the time and space to really consider what our brand was about: to relook at creative strategy, including product, of course, but also all strands of communication and touchpoints, from tone of voice all the way through to projects like our catwalk shows and then *Chubby Hearts* and *Chubby Clouds* and the *Weave Project* and so on. Leading those projects definitely did give me a huge thrill.

Eight years later, in 2019, I realised that, much as I loved being able to focus entirely on the creative, I loved even more leading my own team. I didn't like not running my own company. In 2011, I had thought that I wanted to move to a place where I had less responsibility. I thought I was making the right decision for the business and for myself. But even then I think I knew, somewhere, that I was kind of acting the 'business woman taking on investment' part I thought I should be playing. I wasn't listening to the inner voice asking me whether this was really what I wanted to do. I wasn't being true to myself.

By 2019, I finally understood (and I am sure my children and my husband would ask: 'How did it take you this long?') that I like to be in charge. I like the pressure, I like the adrenalin, I like being the decision-maker. I don't want the quiet life. I not only understood this, I accepted it. I also had the lovely realisation that I knew more than I'd thought. In 2011, part of me felt we needed someone better than me – more experienced, with more formal training – to lead the company. By 2019, I realised that I didn't feel that any more. I think it is a classic mistake that founders make: to think that, just because they started the business without experience and perhaps haven't worked in other businesses, they need a 'professional'. If you can start and grow a business, with all the complexities and sacrifices and tenacity and financial dexterity that requires, then you can cope with most things a business can throw at you. Plus, founders often give heart and soul to a business in a way no one else can, which in turn delivers loyalty and commitment.

Since I took back the role of CEO, with the help of my wonderful new business partners, I am so much happier.

All of this is not to say for a single second that you are not still working on yourself. Of course, even as you create a life that includes as much as possible of what makes you happy, you will still do a million things outside your comfort zone. I still push myself; I still go to all the work events because I meet interesting people and make interesting connections there. I still make myself do public speaking because I have things I want to say and I love to learn from the feedback I get. I still want to work through things that don't feel natural because that's how you develop and learn.

But the point is that I no longer feel bad if I don't enjoy them. I accept that that just isn't me. I accept that it's going to come with some discomfort. It's not my favourite trainers or my comfy coat. And that acceptance, for me, has been an important part of growing up.

<u>There is nothing cooler than the person who is genuinely just happy in their own skin.</u> I am underlining

this because it is important. They know what they are about. They are not trying to be something they're not.

I am thinking about one of my girlfriends who has her own authentic style. She has never given a damn about the latest fashion fads but is incredibly well read and speaks her mind backed up with a combination of knowledge and curiosity. In the nicest possible way, she holds the room. Or one of my male friends who is not stereotypically good-looking. He sits in the pool bare-chested, without a care for his absent six-pack. Women hang on to his every word because he is authoritative, interesting as well as interested, and kind. In fact, we have asked his wife, many times, to leave him to one of us in her will.

These people are truly undoubting, truly confident. They have a style all of their own. They don't care what the magazines say their houses, careers, families or bodies should look like. I so admire and envy these doubt-free, confident people. If you can be happy with your lot and feel lucky with your life, you are the coolest girl in the room.

I am working hard on being that doubt-free person not just some of the time but all of the time. I know there's an irony here: working hard to be someone who is happy with what they have and who they are. But the truth is, this is work for me: I have to work at acknowledging what I am good at; accepting, rather than being annoyed about, those parts of me that are never going to change; and continuing to work on what I can change.

I am prepared now to say that yes, I am good at communicating, and having ideas, and making them happen. I am good at parking (!), most of the time I have nice hair and I can read a room.

And, for example, I have made my peace with the fact that I have a big nose and (mostly) with the fact that I'm never going to have legs like Karlie Kloss.

I spent a lot of my life wishing I was louder and more sociable, but I know that I am actually a borderline introvert/extrovert. Hence not liking big parties and not being able to spend my weekends madly socialising. I wish that someone had said to me early on in life that it's OK to be that person, to be quiet, to need time on my own. I read *Quiet* by Susan Cain and found it really helpful. (Or, to be completely honest, I read the SparkNotes, because, being a bit dyslexic, I am guilty of skim-reading books.) You don't need to be the noisiest, or the coolest, or the funniest person in the room to be interesting.

I have accepted my slightly dyslexic brain. It made me feel stupid and ashamed at school and for years afterwards but now I positively embrace it. I think it is part of what made me so restless in the classroom, so impatient to leave education and just get on with things. And I think it is part of the reason I see things a lot people can't see. I can digest an image immediately and effortlessly – I can close my eyes and tell you exactly what is in the room – whereas text takes me just that bit longer. Visual memory is a much stronger muscle for me than looking at ink on a page. I think it also helps me to communicate simply: I don't like to over-complicate things. And it got me used to feeling a bit lonely and different. All of that has given me advantages in my career and helped me to become who I am.

And, for example, I am still working on . . . well, a million things. I still do dominoes way too much. I am still working on my relationships with exercise and with food. I am still quite intolerant, especially of disorganised or messy people.

I am not saying that, just because you find your authentic self, you're done. I'm not saying that once you find your happy self you stop improving and experimenting and exploring. That's not it at all. We need to keep pushing, to keep developing and growing. I'm saying that once you know – and are prepared to accept – who you are, you can tweak your life to include more of what you love, and you no longer need to endlessly feel bad about what you don't love. And that is golden.

9

How Many More Christmases?

There's a photo in our bathroom that I look at but never notice, as you do when something is in front of your eyes every day. It's a picture of the seven of us on the beach with another family of close friends who also happen to have five children, all jumping in the air. It was the last day of our holiday together and we had decided to take a photo to mark the moment. We took quite a lot of trouble over that photo. I asked everyone to wear white and blue, we positioned ourselves against a beautiful backdrop and we managed to get everyone airborne at the same time. It's just a lovely picture of a happy moment.

About three or four years ago I had a jolt when I suddenly noticed the picture again. I thought: *Was that the moment? Was that the peak?* On the beach, jumping in the air, I was actually worrying about a dozen things. We were on a lovely holiday but we also had five young children and a business to run and we were in the thick of it, exhausted and struggling much of the time. But also it was a moment of pure joy. Since then my children have grown up. Some of them have already left home, beginning to make their own lives. So, was that it? Was it the high point?

I've thought about it a lot since. I actually don't think it was. Or at least I hope it wasn't. It was definitely *a* high point, but there have been high points before and since. What I mean to say is that high points happen without you even realising; it's only when you look back that you can see them for what they were. I am never going to get to some magic moment when I am entirely free of worries, and life would be boring if I did. So now I am trying to recognise, in the moment, when I'm hitting the high points, rather than only appreciating them retrospectively.

I try to think, as I'm getting grumpy over wrapping the presents and finishing work emails before Christmas, and just want to be allowed to sit on the sofa with a glass of wine for five minutes to let all the year's bruises come out: *How many more Christmases do I actually have left? And how do I want to spend them?*

Because, whether I have peaked or not, I am definitely now at least halfway there. I find it hard to believe: I think deep in my subconscious I am still thirty-five years old. I often have a dream just before I wake up, and in the course of my dream, in some half-awake, dreamlike state,

I am slowly becoming conscious, and my thought process is: *OK, who am I? Oh, I like my life. I like my husband. My kids are OK. It's Monday. I'm thirty-five* . . . And then it comes to me as a bolt out of the blue that I am fifty-two. As if time has jumped forward.

Once I have got over the shock, I find it energising: scary but mostly exciting. I'm not thirty-five with a child on each hip. I'm through the tunnel of babies and toddlers and school runs and school plays and parents' evenings. I'm the age of prime ministers, for goodness' sake. I'm a proper grown-up, terrifying as that thought is. But apparently I am one. I've got to the point in my career where I know myself and trust myself: I trust my ability to run a business, to pick a team, to grasp an opportunity, to crack on and hopefully make a difference. I've got to the point in my life where I know what really matters to me. This decade, between fifty and sixty, this is my time, and I have to make it count. It feels a bit like when you reach the halfway point on a holiday. The fog lifts, and you start to get focused on what you haven't done and what you need to achieve in the time you have left.

As you might expect by now, there's a list for this. A visualisation. I have a wish list of things I can imagine getting to the end of my life and regretting not having done. In my dreams, I would like to go to every continent with my family. I would love to see the Seven Wonders of the Modern World and the amazing sunken churches in Ethiopia. It would be incredible to visit Persepolis and Cappadocia and wake up early to witness the great migration of wildebeest in the Masai Mara. I would like to try to sing again. I would love to design and build a beautiful garden. There's so much I want to see and do, so please God can we work out a way to travel that doesn't damage the planet while I am still relatively young.

My advice is this: write a list of your own. Big things, small things, things you want to do, places you want to see, skills you want to gain, things you want to come to terms with, people you want to reconcile with. Otherwise, if you're not careful, it will all slide by and before you know it you will be eighty-five and suddenly it won't be so easy to pull it all off.

*

I have come to understand what really matters gradually, as I have aged, and suddenly, through the trauma of my son being ill. And just when I thought I had made sense of it enough to write about it, along came Covid-19, forcing me to take a harder look.

Being ill with something life-threatening must be almost the worst thing that can happen to a person. And having a child who is ill with something life-threatening is certainly one of the worst things that can happen to a parent.

My oldest son, Hugo, went off to university aged nineteen and during the Christmas holidays I noticed a mole on his back. It looked a little bit odd and I asked him to get it checked, but I didn't for a second think it was anything to worry about. I should have made more of a fuss to push him to do it, but I suppose I just didn't think it was that serious – we are a very moley family. Well, he was nineteen and he had other priorities. He went back to university and didn't get it checked. A couple of months later, though, he called me and mentioned he had pulled a muscle rowing and was going to the doctor. I asked him to show the doctor his mole while he was there.

The next time he called, he said to us something like, 'By the way, I showed the doctor the mole. They've cut it off and they're going to biopsy it.' We were a bit worried but we hoped this was just a sensible, precautionary measure and that it would come back benign.

A week later we went to visit. It was Eights Week, a big, rowdy, joyful summer rowing event at the university. Crowds of students were gathered on the riverbanks in their college colours, shouting for their teams. The weather was glorious. Hugo was out there on the river, rowing for his college, and we were very proud and happy to be there to witness it. After his race – which he won – he came up to join us on the noisy viewing platform of the boathouse and we gave him a big hug. It was then that he told us (rather casually) that he had just had a call from the dermatologist to say that the biopsy result had come back and it was a melanoma. 'But they don't know whether it's spread. They need to do more tests.'

Those are the moments when life stops. All around us people were drinking summer drinks and excitedly greeting friends and family. We said something like, 'Hugo, hang on, what?' And then he was called over by his friends to watch the next race.

James and I were left reeling. It was hard to take it in and the world immediately took on an unreal quality that stayed with us for years.

Because Hugo was already twenty, we realised all the communications for appointments and so on were going to come directly to him. We said, 'Obviously it's up to you, because you're an adult, but if it's OK with you we want to be involved in everything. Like, absolutely everything. Because what happens to you happens to us.' And he kindly agreed.

And then we had to wait to find out whether it had spread. That wait is the worst, as anyone who has been through it knows. This first time, we all stayed at home and cut ourselves off. We didn't know what to do with ourselves. The results came back. It hadn't spread, but he needed urgent surgery to remove the lump and they would know more after that.

How could this be happening to us? How could it happen to my twenty-year-old boy, who was so fit and healthy and gorgeous? How was this fair: to lose your mother at four and then to get cancer at twenty?

In the end, we learnt that what we actually needed to do in those waiting times was to continue completely as normal. Every time we had another scare and another biopsy, we religiously and with huge discipline forced ourselves to carry on with our normal lives: if not in our heads – because that was impossible – then in outward appearance, as far as we could.

Hugo had surgery, and then more surgery. Just as we were approaching the five-years-clear mark, he phoned us to say he had found a new lump and, a week later, to say, 'It's come back for round two.' I will never forget that phone call. More biopsies, more hideous waits. It had spread but only locally, thank goodness. More surgery. Our doctor and the whole medical team were amazing. Hugo was so brave, and so impressive. Frankly, he took my breath away. He never once did the 'poor me' thing I would certainly have done in his situation and he just kept on going. They decided to give him a brand-new treatment called ipilimumab, a form of immunotherapy that had been developed in the time between the first melanoma and this latest episode, together with very targeted radiotherapy. It worked. Thank God for our brilliant scientists.

When something like this happens to you, you understand how out of control you are. And you brace.

Because when you get the call saying it's melanoma, it's the biggest punch in the stomach you can ever have. And then you are so scared of being punched again that you remain braced. It feels too dangerous to relax and make yourself vulnerable because you can't take another blow like that. It's safer to stay prepped and ready.

It has taken years but finally we have allowed ourselves, little by little, to let go and un-brace. We had a really happy surprise party for Hugo when he reached the four-years-clear mark, because that is a major milestone in terms of risk. He now, aged thirty-one, finally has the same prognosis as any normal person his age. Touch wood and *Deo gratias*.

It was a terrible time – the worst time – and yet, amazingly, there were quite a few silver linings. It seems inappropriate to talk of silver linings when discussing a child being ill, but I think anyone who has been through this will acknowledge that they exist. They are much-needed when you are in the thick of it, so my advice is to grab them with both hands.

If I am writing a note now to someone who is going through what we went through, or sitting and talking to someone, I'll say, 'Don't feel guilty about claiming those silver linings. They are what you're given as a sort of consolation prize. And you might as well take them. In fact, embrace them and hold on tight, because, blimey, you need them.'

One silver lining for us was that the three of us became very close. We did all the medical things together because that was the only way we could manage. And we did a lot of talking. We developed a ritual where we would go and see the consultant and then, whatever the news, we would have lunch or dinner in a tapas bar near the hospital. Tapas and a glass of sherry to take the edge off. And actually those moments, facing it all together, were special. Around the time that we found out that the cancer had spread but only locally, not to the lymph nodes, the three of us were walking to a pizza restaurant one evening and Hugo said, 'You know what, through this whole period, one thing I've learnt is, I've understood the meaning of family.' What a thing to say. What an incredible silver lining.

The other, and biggest, silver lining was the sense of perspective I gained. I remember sitting in one of those awful hospital rooms waiting for Hugo to come back from surgery and understanding that none of what I had previously thought were my problems actually mattered very much. In the days running up to that moment in the college boathouse, I was *so* stressed with this and that, and *so* flat out, and *so* busy. But in the weeks and months and years that followed – years of hell – I understood that those problems I was so eaten up by were just part of the delicious game of chess that is normal life. Was this person going to leave the company? Would that order get delivered? Would we make a margin on this product? These problems were simply what filled my days. They were real problems and they made up the fabric of my life and they made me feel relevant, meaningful, needed, justified. But they were absolutely golden, frankly, compared to what we were going through. I couldn't wait to go back to those being my problems. The only things that really matter are the ones that come out of nowhere: the phone call that makes you drop everything and run for the car. The rest is just a way of getting through life, so try to get through it in the best way you can.

Ultimately, I realised, from afar we are all just lots of little ants scurrying this way and that, up and down, looking very busy and feeling very important. And we need those things in our lives that make us feel busy and important; we need wants and drive and ambitions; we need to feel like it all matters. But actually, most of it is just there to keep us busy and stop us being bored. When the chips are down, most of it doesn't matter. So we have to try to keep all of that scurrying in perspective and not take it too seriously.

Once you have faced a really big health scare or a hideous bereavement, all the 'wiggly ant problems' look different. You realise, one way or another, that you are going to come through this problem and get to the end of it. It might be good or it might be bad, and of course we really hope it's good, but somehow you will get through it. For Hugo himself, I felt that he had faced two of the worst things a person could possibly have to face in the course of his first twenty years and come through them. If he managed that, he could manage anything. He had nothing to be scared of any more.

(I have to just add here: at one point when we were sitting on the ward with Hugo, our lovely surgeon said, 'You know, there are four other boys Hugo's age on the same ward, all going through the same thing.' So please, put suncream on your kids. Don't let them go out in the midday sun. Make them wear a T-shirt. The tan is just not worth it.)

*

I always knew family was important to me but I didn't understand how much my parents had done for me until I had children myself. And I hadn't anticipated the next shift either: that moment when you realise that you need to start to take care of your parents, or parents-in-law, as they once took care of you.

I remember watching that shift happen to my own mother with my grandfather. My mother is an only child and when her mother died, her father was not equipped to look after himself. My grandmother had always done the cooking and managed the home. Overnight, my mother had to step into being a full-on carer for him. It was hard for her to delegate because, naturally, what he wanted was for his daughter to be there for him. She prepared all his meals, organised all his washing. It was tough on top of managing her own young family.

My parents are still fit and healthy. But when my mother-in-law started to become forgetful and less able to look after herself, we all felt quite scared. She was widowed and so she lived on her own, in Wiltshire, two hours away from us. We were worried she would trip, we were worried she wouldn't eat. She couldn't manage FaceTime or similar methods of communication that would have meant we could see her as well as speak to her, so it was hard to really know how she was doing unless we were physically there. She then had a health setback and we had to intervene as she was worryingly underweight. We divided the tasks among the siblings and the role that James and I took on was organising her care. We found a local agency who could pop in twice a day, prep meals, shop and so on, but mainly just keep an eye. This worked for a bit but it soon became clear that it was not enough. She was vulnerable and it was a huge worry for everyone. On reflection, it is a source of shame for me that, rather than letting her decide how she wanted to move forward to the next stage, we, in a caring but let's-get-it-organised kind of way, sorted it all out for her. We found live-in carers, and I wrote up a lot of notes saying 'This is how you put out the rubbish' and 'This is what Liz likes for lunch' and 'Lunch should be at one o'clock.' While it was clearly going to keep her safe and stop us worrying, in retrospect it was possibly invasive and insensitive. I didn't at first realise that in our attempt to be kind and to make it all work we were actually disempowering and infantilising my lovely mother-in-law. A bit of me thinks that in my anxiety to make it work, and my guilt that we couldn't be there ourselves, I was focused more on getting it covered and not enough on what Liz perhaps wanted. I understand now, thanks to a wonderful book by the doctor Atul Gawande, that I should have allowed her to stay in control. The moment you let a person feel they're not in control any more, that's when they really age and really decline. Of course it came out of all the right instincts of safety and love, but it is something I think about a lot now.

I have cherished my relationships with my girlfriends more and more as I get older. That isn't only because my husband is twelve years older than me, although it would be typical of him to outlive me. It's more because I think girlfriends matter more as you get older. Quite simply, my girlfriends make me happy. They are interesting, interested, smart and brilliant women. They have always been loyal, kind and by my side when I needed them. I was constantly amazed by the support and help of my girlfriends during the sometimes fraught process of buying my business back. Their company nourishes me, and one of my great pleasures as I get older is to spend more time with them. We often laugh about creating a commune when we are old wizened widows.

Exercise. Well, yes, exercise and I still have a love-hate relationship, but what I have come to understand is that, as you approach fifty, suddenly health is the only game in town. I spent the first few decades of my life pursuing a series of different goals: I wanted a good education, I wanted friends, I wanted a boyfriend, I wanted to build a business, I wanted to get married, I wanted a home, I wanted children. And then, somewhere around forty-seven, I started looking at fifty and I realised that everything had shifted. Those things still all mattered. But from here on, the biggest goal was to be healthy, or else I was going to have zero fun as I got older. Doctors refer to the years between the ages of fifty and sixty as 'sniper alley'. If you haven't been looking after yourself up until now, you need to start. If you've been looking after yourself, you need to ramp it up. If you aren't fifty yet, that's wonderful. Exercise anyway. Get ahead, get money in the bank for later. It's like paying into a pension: if you want to enjoy your old age, you have to invest now, and the earlier you start the better.

Ageing must be hardest for the beautiful people as they have the most to lose. I was really struck once when my mother-in-law said that as she reached old age she became 'invisible'. If beauty is your North Star, ageing will be very depressing. But in truth, the losses hit all of us and we all have to adjust. The first time I caught sight of my own droopy eyelid was a moment, I will grant you. I remember I put on some eyeliner and it transferred onto my eyebrow and I thought, 'Oh. Oh no.' And then (thank you, Nora Ephron) I started to feel bad about my neck and I found myself wearing higher-necked tops and holding my head at an uncomfortable angle to try to stretch the skin out on Zoom calls. I think that your eyesight fading – another gift of getting older – is perhaps just an act of kindness. Of course, I wish now that I had appreciated how amazing my skin was when I had a smooth neck and no smile lines.

I do want to look good as I get older. But I have decided that this is not my next decade's battle. There are limits to what I'm prepared to put into this – limits to how much money and time and energy I'm going to spend on fighting an exhausting fight that I'm never going to win, when the real win is to stay fit and healthy and strong. Plus, some of the most beautiful women I know and admire have wrinkly faces that are true to their age and their life experience. So I will do what is simple and easy and pain-free. I will invest in some good face creams that convince me they can tighten up my eyelids or de-crêpe my décolleté. I will stay out of the sun (ish). But I will not – for now, and let's see how I do sticking to this over the next five years – do too much more. And I'm going to try to convince my core girlfriends to take the same approach, because the moment one of us goes to the next stage, it's harder for the others not to follow. Men seem to grasp this instinctively. Most men have such simple grooming routines: no make-up, no leg waxing, no eyebrow threading; just jump in the shower and that's that. Because none of them play the game, none of them have to play the game. Let's take a leaf out of their book: it's a zero-sum game, so it would great if we all just agreed not to play it.

I think a lot about the planet that I am going to leave behind me. I see the challenges of protecting the planet as this generation's war. I am proud of my children's generation: the people who are telling us that what we have done to the planet is terrible and that we have to step it up. They are right. In our defence, a bit like with smoking, we didn't know the damage we were inflicting until it was almost too late. But it is time to take it very seriously. Covid is scary, but having an unhealthy, inhospitable planet to live on is in another league altogether.

There is a lot that businesses can and should do to help, and within that a lot that the fashion industry can and should do, because we are big and noisy and vocal. But businesses also have to employ people and pay taxes and answer to their shareholders, and if caring for the planet involves a hit to their margins it is often difficult to take that first step.

Customers also have to demand change, and be prepared to pay a bit more for it. Retailers and designers and brands need to realise that they have to meet that demand if they want to keep that generation of customers, and be prepared to accept a slightly lower margin. We need to get to the stage where everyone in the supply chain realises they are only going to get orders and be profitable if they do things in the right way, and give us the responsibly sourced, sustainable, innovative products we need.

Doing our bit doesn't mean being immediately perfect: it means to start to make some changes and seeing where you can make a difference. We are all busy, and it's hard to change, but that is not a reason to do nothing. It's OK if you only do 20 per cent at the beginning, because once you start something you tend to keep going. It's like if you start going to the gym, you tend to start eating more healthily. Let's not criticise everyone for not being perfect – let's instead praise the people who are doing *something* and encourage them to keep it up. Voltaire was right when he wrote that 'the best is the enemy of the good'.

Finally, kindness. My fifty-two years have taught me that not only is it simply the right way to behave, but that it is good for you too. My youngest son's godfather introduced us to the concept of the favour bank. You keep paying in. Maybe it's flowers and a hug for someone who is upset even if you don't know them all that well. Maybe it's finding a good excuse to call someone who is on their own but too proud to say they are lonely. Perhaps you give someone a leg up in their career because they are good and you can. You help someone out of a mess. You give someone a compliment because that's what they need that day. It's those little things you do where you don't expect anything back, which we all do pretty naturally, I hope. You pay in and pay in and pay in. It mostly shouldn't even be a conscious thing but sometimes you have to make the effort. And when you need it, when you've got a problem, it will most likely pay out.

If, on the other hand, you have been unfair or unkind or trodden on others to achieve your success, it's not real success. I am sure there is a connection between being ruthless and being successful, but it's just not the kind of successful I care about. And it's not the kind of successful that, ultimately, makes many people happy. What goes around comes around, albeit often more slowly than one might wish.

*

As I look ahead to the next ten years, I am brought back, often, to the ants. Life is just an ant wiggle. We are all just wiggling our way from the beginning of our lives to the end and trying to do the best we can. The wiggling feels like it matters dreadfully, but ultimately not a lot of it really does. I would love my wiggly line to leave a bit of a mark, to make a difference. I am up for trying. But what really matters is to be healthy, to be kind, and to pass that baton well.

FURTHER READING

On sleep: Russell Foster and Leon Kreitzman, *Circadian Rhythms: A Very Short Introduction* (Oxford University Press, 2017)

On sugar: Professor Julia Buckroyd, *Understanding Your Eating: How to Eat and Not Worry About It* (Open University Press, 2011)

On body image: Emily Clarkson: @em_clarkson on Instagram

On feeling bad about your neck: Nora Ephron, *I Feel Bad About My Neck: And Other Thoughts About Being a Woman* (Doubleday, 2006)

On child bereavement: Julia Samuel, *Grief Works* (Penguin, 2017)

On neuro-linguistic programming: William Scott-Masson's website: williamscottmasson.com

On dyslexia and entrepreneurship: www.cass.city.ac.uk/_ _data/assets/pdf_file/0003/367383/julielogan-dyslexic-entrepreneurs.pdf

On the environment: Anon, *Change the World for a Fiver: We Are What We Do* (Short Books, 2004)

On getting things done: David Allen, *Getting Things Done: The Art of Stress-Free Productivity* (Piatkus, 2001), and next-action.co.uk

On decluttering: Gill Hasson, *Declutter Your Life: How Outer Order Leads to Inner Calm* (Capstone, 2017)

On knowing yourself: 16personalities.com

On accepting yourself: Susan Cain, *Quiet: The Power of Introverts in a World That Can't Stop Talking* (Penguin, 2012)

On being blindsided on a Tuesday afternoon and other excellent advice: Mary Schmich, 'Advice, like youth, probably just wasted on the young', aka 'Everybody's Free (To Wear Sunscreen)': www.chicagotribune.com/columns/chi-schmich-sunscreen-column-column.html

On ageing and independence: Atul Gawande, *Being Mortal: Illness, Medicine, and What Matters in the End* (Profile, 2014)

ACKNOWLEDGEMENTS

There are so many people who have so kindly helped me with this book.

I would like to start by thanking the chicest of agents, Caroline Michel who pushed me to do this and who kindly introduced me to Deborah Crewe without whom I certainly couldn't have done it.

Caroline also introduced me to the Editor of Editors, Alexis Kirschbaum, who brought with her the 'Bloomsbury A-Team': Jasmine Horsey, Emma Ewbank, Rachel Wilkie, Genista Tate-Alexander, Lauren Whybrow and Nicola Hill. You are all legends and I am so grateful for going the extra mile (and then some).

Same for Sarah Bennie who is also a legend.

Thank you to my team AH, most especially the brilliant Kate and Matt and, of course, Imy.

Thank you to 'other' Kate R, Sarah S and Christiane A for reading this and giving honest feedback. It takes real friends to be honest.

Thank you to Hugo for being my 'in-family' lawyer and for allowing me to share his brave story.

Thank you to Tia for her help with 'the saga of chapter one' and also Bert.

Sorry to Felix and Otto for always working on the book at the weekend.

Thank you to my incredible parents for teaching me much of what I have written about.

And finally, *no thanks* to James (for the book) but thank you for feeding me and pretending to listen. I would never admit this publicly but I love you very much.

Anya

A NOTE ON THE AUTHOR

Anya Hindmarch founded her company as a teenager in 1987. She has since grown it into an award-winning global brand known for its craftsmanship, creativity and sense of humour, including the hugely successful 'I'm Not A Plastic Bag' campaign. An advocate of British design and arts, Anya is NED of the British Fashion Council and Emeritus Trustee of the Royal Academy of Arts and the Design Museum. She was appointed Governor of the University of the Arts in 2010 and a Prime Minister's Business Ambassador in 2011, holds both an MBE and a CBE and is a Trustee of the Royal Marsden Cancer Charity. She has honorary doctorates from the Universities of East Anglia and Essex but lives in London, where her proudest achievement is hosting a sleepover in the bed department of Peter Jones.